Optimal Spending on Cybersecurity Measures

This book explores the strategic decisions made by organizations when implementing cybersecurity controls and leveraging economic models and theories from the economics of information security and risk-management frameworks.

Based on unique and distinct research completed within the field of risk management and information security, this book provides insight into organizational risk-management processes utilized in determining cybersecurity investments. It describes how theoretical models and frameworks rely on either specific scenarios or controlled conditions and how decisions on cybersecurity spending within organizations—specifically, the funding available in comparison to the recommended security measures necessary for compliance—vary depending on stakeholders. As the trade-off between the costs of implementing a security measure and the benefit derived from the implementation of security controls is not easily measured, a business leader's decision to fund security measures may be biased. The author presents an innovative approach to assess cybersecurity initiatives with a risk-management perspective and leverages a data-centric focus on the evolution of cyber-attacks.

This book is ideal for business school students and technology professionals with an interest in risk management.

Tara Kissoon is a multi-certified IT Risk & Security Leader with more than 20 years of experience in technology and 13 years of experience in the financial services industry. She brings continued success to technology, IT risk and information security programmes and projects within large organizations. She is acknowledged as a leader, security architect and trusted advisor with a talent for working with cross-functional teams to achieve short- and long-term business objectives.

Routledge Focus on Business and Management

The fields of business and management have grown exponentially as areas of research and education. This growth presents challenges for readers trying to keep up with the latest important insights. *Routledge Focus on Business and Management* presents small books on big topics and how they intersect with the world of business research.

Individually, each title in the series provides coverage of a key academic topic, whilst collectively, the series forms a comprehensive collection across the business disciplines.

Creating Business and Corporate Strategy
An Integrated Strategic System
Adyl Aliekperov

Crony Capitalism in US Health Care
Anatomy of a Dysfunctional System
Naresh Khatri

Entrepreneurship Education
Scholarly Progress and Future Challenges
Gustav Hägg and Agnieszka Kurczewska

Culture and Resilience at Work
A Study of Stress and Hardiness among Indian Corporate Professionals
Pallabi Mund

Optimal Spending on Cybersecurity Measures
Risk Management
Tara Kissoon

For more information about this series, please visit: www.routledge.com/Routledge-Focus-on-Business-and-Management/book-series/FBM

Optimal Spending on Cybersecurity Measures

Risk Management

Tara Kissoon

Routledge
Taylor & Francis Group

LONDON AND NEW YORK

First published 2022
by Routledge
2 Park Square, Milton Park, Abingdon, Oxon OX14 4RN

and by Routledge
605 Third Avenue, New York, NY 10158

Routledge is an imprint of the Taylor & Francis Group, an informa business

© 2022 Tara Kissoon

British Library Cataloguing-in-Publication Data
A catalogue record for this book is available from the British Library

Library of Congress Cataloging-in-Publication Data
Names: Kissoon, Tara, author.
Title: Optimal spending on cybersecurity measures : risk management / Tara Kissoon.
Description: Abingdon, Oxon ; New York, NY : Routledge, 2022. | Series: Routledge focus on business and management | Includes bibliographical references and index.
Identifiers: LCCN 2021015074 (print) | LCCN 2021015075 (ebook)
Subjects: LCSH: Data protection. | Computer security. | Computer networks—Security measures. | Risk management.
Classification: LCC HF5548.37 .K57 2022 (print) | LCC HF5548.37 (ebook) | DDC 658.4/78—dc23
LC record available at https://lccn.loc.gov/2021015074
LC ebook record available at https://lccn.loc.gov/2021015075

ISBN: 978-1-032-06140-5 (hbk)
ISBN: 978-1-032-06141-2 (pbk)
ISBN: 978-1-003-20089-5 (ebk)

DOI: 10.4324/9781003200895

Typeset in Times New Roman
by Apex CoVantage, LLC

Content

Preface

The aim of this book is to discuss the decision-making process for cybersecurity investments in organizations using a conceptual cybersecurity risk-management framework. Most conceptual models consider the dynamic environment, which is adaptable to changes that occur within the decision-making process. These models and frameworks rely on either specific scenarios or controlled conditions. As a result of the dynamic environment within the cybersecurity industry, mitigation strategies evolve to address emerging industry threats. These variations influence the conditions that were used within previous frameworks and economic models. Decisions regarding cybersecurity spending within organizations vary based on the stakeholders—specifically, the funding available in comparison to the recommended security measures necessary for compliance. These executive decisions may be coloured with bias regarding the appropriate security baseline required to protect relevant information assets within the organization. The trade-off between the costs of implementing a security measure and the benefit derived from the implementation is not easily measured. Therefore, the lack of this information may impact the business leader's decision to fund security measures and the choice to further invest in developing new technology to drive innovation, business growth and customer satisfaction.

This book focuses on the strategic decisions made by organizations when implementing cybersecurity measures and belongs to the area of risk management, leveraging various models within the fields of (1) economics, (2) organizational decision-making and (3) cybersecurity to determine optimal spending on cybersecurity measures, which includes a preventative approach for risk-taking organizations. This book provides a cybersecurity risk-management framework and demonstrates the application of the process using case studies. This book discusses risk-management practices in organizations and defines a strategic approach to minimize cybersecurity risks.

This book makes an industry contribution by assisting business leaders with choosing an appropriate risk-mitigation strategy when implementing cybersecurity measures. The application of this framework within organizations will assist stakeholders with decisions pertaining to cybersecurity spending. In leveraging the review of additional studies, this book aims to utilize a case study methodology to demonstrate that risk-based decisions are necessary when implementing cybersecurity measures. The case study methodology provides an in-depth view of a risk-taking organization's risk-mitigation strategy within the bounds of an educational environment focusing on the following five areas identified within a digital cyber risk model: (1) technology landscape, (2) data classification, (3) risk-management practices, (4) cost–benefit analysis for cybersecurity measures and (5) business objectives.

1 Introduction

Introduction

This book shares a strategic framework that could be used by the various stakeholders involved in the implementation of cybersecurity measures to safeguard sensitive data. The existing literature shows that a wide range of principles are relevant within the cybersecurity decision-making process. Specific security measures are important and should be implemented appropriately to alleviate cybersecurity threats. The information provided in this book gives the necessary data to show that the cybersecurity decision-making process is clearly integrated with risk-management methodologies and the economics of information security to include current opportunity cost models.

Economic optimization of information security is an area of interest to researchers and executives in most organizations. From a financial viewpoint, cost–benefit analysis is necessary and impactful to justify cybersecurity spending, as it relates to security measures. Previous authors have focused on either traditional risk-management practices or the organizational decision-making process of information security investments using cost–benefit analysis.

This book aims to discuss the integration of organizational decision-making within cybersecurity spending to effectively articulate the business impact of cybersecurity risks. It focuses on the integration of risk-management practices with economics to support a balanced approach to cyber risk management. Each area was reviewed in-depth to provide an understanding of its application to cybersecurity and the decision-making process used when evaluating and investing in various security measures. Three global industry areas were analysed to gain a further understanding of current gaps, as noted later.

DOI: 10.4324/9781003200895-1

Why are current implementations of cybersecurity frameworks effective in identifying, monitoring and responding to cybersecurity threats?

In analysing industry data, it is apparent that organizations currently leverage government and industry frameworks when implementing cybersecurity measures. The foundation of the decisions made by most stakeholders is based on ensuring compliance with government regulations, industry standards and internal policy.

In addition, most organizations have anonymously expressed that they have experienced a type of cybersecurity breach, prioritized as follows: (1) malware/ransomware, (2) phishing, (3) lost/stolen computer media and (4) external/data breach, where 94% of respondents expressed an average dollar loss of between $0 and $1 million. Organizational stakeholders believe that they can detect, respond to and monitor a security incident; however, they are not able to continuously prevent security incidents from occurring within their environment.

These stakeholders believe that their organization is in compliance with government and industry standards. An organization measures the effectiveness of the implemented cybersecurity framework according to the following priorities: (1) compliance, (2) audit/assurance testing, (3) key performance indicators (KPIs), (4) capacity maturity models and (5) cost, considering the organization's risk profile.

What factors are used by an organization when investing in cybersecurity controls?

The decision-making mechanisms utilized by organizations when evaluating and implementing different security measures primarily focus on (1) compliance with government and industry regulations, (2) investment cost, (3) the impact of either a breach or fine, (4) either reputational or brand risk and (5) ease of use by the business.

What decision-making mechanisms are organizations using when evaluating different security measures prior to implementation?

Stakeholders that make decisions on cybersecurity measures within their organizations include the following: (1) Chief Technology Officer (CTO), (2) Chief Information Security Officer (CISO), (3) Head of Business Line, (4) Chief Information Officer (CIO) and (5) Board of Directors. The CTO and CISO are the stakeholders primarily responsible for advising and funding the investments within their organization, and each organization's investment budget is between $1 and $5 million annually. Stakeholders are involved during the implementation of cybersecurity measures in the following ways: (1) direct involvement in the decision-making mechanism, (2) attendance at meetings on evaluating cybersecurity measures, (3) involvement in implementation activities related to cybersecurity measures and (4) support of the cybersecurity function.

It is apparent that organizations have actively implemented cybersecurity frameworks; however, there is a need to enhance the decision-making process to reduce the number and types of breaches while strengthening the implemented cybersecurity framework to facilitate a stronger preventative approach. In addition, the factors used by an organization when investing in cybersecurity controls are heavily focused on compliance with government and industry regulations. Last, the decision-making process utilized when evaluating, implementing and investing in cybersecurity controls is weighted towards the technology organization and, therefore, may be biased based on competing priorities.

Most organizations are faced with an array of choices when deciding on funding, as it relates to cybersecurity measures. Funding the investment cost to provide a secure environment can be complex.

Cost–benefit analyses, risk appetite and business trade-offs are some of the areas that are factored into the overall decision-making process. Most stakeholders indicate that the following areas are critical in an organization's decision-making process when allocating funds for cybersecurity measures.

Allocation of budget

Although stakeholders believe that their organization has allocated a large enough budget to respond to or detect a cybersecurity breach, it is apparent that their organization's cybersecurity budget is insufficient to ensure appropriate cybersecurity measures to prevent such breaches.

Ability to prevent a cybersecurity breach

Although stakeholders believe that their organization can detect a cybersecurity breach in a timely manner, it is apparent that their organization is unable to prevent a cybersecurity breach, as some stakeholders indicate that their organization has encountered more than 15 breaches.

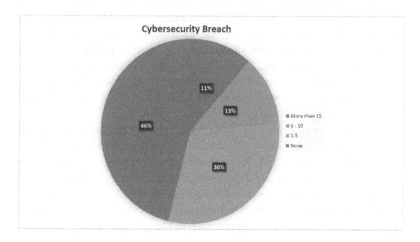

Figure 1.1 Regarding the ability of an organization to prevent a cybersecurity breach, 30% of respondents experienced five or fewer cybersecurity breaches.

Measuring the effectiveness of implemented frameworks

Stakeholders believe that their organization's current information security framework implementation is ineffective in preventing cybersecurity breaches. In addition, it is apparent that most organizations measure the effectiveness of their current information security framework implementation by (1) compliance with policy, (2) audit and assurance testing, (3) KPIs, (4) cost and (5) capacity maturity models.

Risk level

Stakeholders indicate that their organization's decision-making process is aligned with a risk methodology, and as noted within most industry-recognized economic models, this methodology directly impacts the cost–benefit analysis.

Importance of decision-makers

It is apparent in most organizations that the decisions made by the CIO and head of the business line have similar priorities regarding (1) funding the investment cost, (2) implementing information security measures and (3) reviewing the risk appetite statement. This parallel decision-making

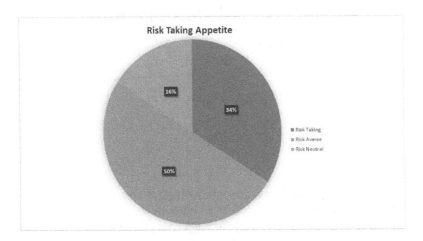

Figure 1.2 Thirty-four percent of organizations have a risk-taking risk appetite (Kissoon, 2020).

process may have an adverse impact on the decision to fund cybersecurity measures, especially in circumstances where the viewpoints are vastly different.

This book examines risk-management practices and applicable frameworks to define an appropriate cyber risk investment model.

2 Enterprise risk-management framework

Risk-management methodologies stem from the enterprise risk-management (ERM) framework. This is defined as an organization's ability to understand, control and articulate the nature and level of risks taking into account the business strategy, coupled with accountability for organizational risk. One of the main benefits of the ERM framework is an enhanced viewpoint and focus on risk management within the organization.

ERM addresses the following organizational questions:

- Should we pursue this initiative? This aligns with strategy, risk appetite, culture and ethics.
- Can we achieve this initiative? This aligns with people, processes, structure and technological capabilities—that is, operational risk.
- Did we accomplish this initiative? This is the assessment of expected results, continuous learning and a robust system of checks and balances.

ERM promotes strategies that assist organizations in holistically managing risk. ERM is a governance structure that provides a horizontal view of the risk disciplines and operational risks of an institution.

Figure 2.1 The COSO Internal Control Framework (COSO, 2020).

DOI: 10.4324/9781003200895-2

The elements of the ERM framework are detailed in the following sections.

Internal environment

Management determines the philosophy regarding risk and establishes the level of risk the organization is willing to assume, known as risk appetite. The internal control environment provides the basis of how risk and controls are assessed and managed by an organization. The importance of ERM is communicated by executive management throughout the organization.

Common language around risk

The risk-management approach must involve establishing a common risk terminology with appropriate training and awareness of the terminology by stakeholders within the organization. A common definition of risk is "the potential for loss, or the diminished opportunity for gain, which can obstruct the achievement of an organization's business objectives". Common terminology will facilitate communication across business units:

- Risk is the possibility that an event will occur and adversely affect the achievement of objectives.
- Risk culture is the appearance of ERM and the attitude towards it that management conveys to the organization's personnel. Are management actions aligned with the implemented ERM strategies?" (COSO, 2020).

Risk-management steering committee

It is important to establish a senior management-level committee to provide oversight of the implementation of the ERM framework. In addition, the committee will help delineate roles, responsibilities and accountabilities as identified within the framework.

> *Roles and responsibilities:* They must be clearly defined and communicated throughout an organization.
>
> *Board of directors and CEO*: They have ultimate accountability for all risks. Risk-management practices must be discussed periodically, and risk-management-related policies must be reviewed and approved.
>
> *Senior management*: Senior managers are responsible for designing, implementing and maintaining an effective framework. In addition, they

should develop policies and procedures, establish and monitor the risk appetite level and report regularly to the board of directors.

Business units: They (1) promote a risk-aware culture; (2) identify, (3) assess, (4) measure, (5) monitor, (6) control and (7) report risks to senior management; (8) manage relevant risks within the framework established by senior management; and (9) ensure compliance with policies and procedures.

Support departments—that is, legal, HR, and information technology (IT): They provide support to business units in developing and enforcing policies and procedures.

Internal audit and compliance: They monitor and provide independent assurance of the effectiveness of the framework.

Risk management: Risk managers coordinate the establishment of the framework and provide expertise.

Objective setting

Objectives must exist before management can identify potential events affecting the achievement of organizational goals. ERM ensures that management has a process in place to set objectives and that the chosen objectives support and are aligned and consistent with an organization's mission and risk appetite.

ERM methodology

The development of a methodology for the ERM framework should include definitions of key risk terms, descriptions of roles and responsibilities and clear procedures for risk identification, assessment, measurement, mitigation, monitoring and reporting. The methodology should be expressed in a formally written document that comprises all the key business areas. The document should consider the organization's strategic direction and objectives and clearly outline its capacity to take risks and its tolerance of potential loss. In addition, the risk appetite level must be regularly reviewed and approved by the senior management and board of directors.

Risk appetite

Risk appetite is the amount of risk, on a broad level, that an organization is willing to accept as it tries to achieve its goals and provide value to stakeholders. It reflects the ERM philosophy and in turn influences the organization's culture and operating style.

Risk tolerance

Risk tolerance is the acceptable level of variation relative to the achievement of a specific objective and is often measured using the same units as the related objective. In setting risk tolerance, management considers the relative importance of the related objective and aligns risk tolerance with risk appetite to ensure that it operates within its risk appetite level.

Event identification

Potential events from internal or external sources that might have an impact on the organization and affect the achievement of its objectives must be identified. Event identification includes distinguishing between events that represent risks, those that represent opportunities and those that may represent both risks and opportunities.

Risk assessment

The identified risks are analysed and associated with objectives that may be affected to form a basis for determining how they should be managed. Risks are assessed on both inherent and residual bases, and the assessment should consider both risk likelihood and impact. Risk assessment must be performed continuously and throughout an organization.

Quantitative risk assessment

Quantitative risk assessment refers to attempts to assign a monetary value to the assets being assessed, a monetary cost to the impact of an adverse event and percentages to the frequency of threats and the likelihood of events.

Risk calculation

Risk = Asset Value × Threat × Vulnerability

Asset value is usually the easiest to measure; however, it is difficult to quantify certain assets, such as institutional reputation.

Threat may be very difficult to measure the potential for harm, although information from external sources is useful.

Vulnerability can be measured using automated computing device vulnerability tools to provide information, but not all vulnerabilities can be quantified.

Qualitative risk assessment

Qualitative risk assessments are scenario driven and do not attempt to assign monetary value to the assets being assessed or to the impact of an adverse event. They aim to rank the impacts of threats and criticality of assets into categories such as low, medium and high.

Risk response

The organization identifies and evaluates possible responses to risks, which include avoiding, accepting, reducing and sharing risks. Management selects a set of actions to align risks with the organization's risk tolerance and risk appetite. The ERM framework advocates the following responses:

- Avoidance means the organization ceases the activities that cause the risk. Some examples of avoidance are ending a product line, selling a division or deciding against expansion.
- Reduction means action is taken to mitigate the risk likelihood and impact.
- Sharing means reducing the risk likelihood and impact by sharing a proportion of the risk. An extremely common sharing response is insurance.
- Acceptance means no action is taken to affect the risk likelihood or impact.

Control activities

Policies and procedures are established and implemented to ensure that the risk responses selected by management are effectively carried out.

Risk identification

Risk identification can be completed through a risk control self-assessment (RCSA) approach coordinated by risk management and conducted with subject-matter experts. This method uses a risk taxonomy to identify applicable risks, inherent risk levels, quality of internal controls and residual risk levels.

The process consists of the following steps:

- Identify applicable risks and describe the business activity that exposes the business unit to each risk.
- Establish the inherent risk level *(H, M, L)* and typical annual damage. Inherent risk prevents the achievement of business objectives without considering internal controls. Typical annual damage, if applicable,

can be estimated based on the subjective judgement of the business unit and should consider both past (actual losses) and potential future occurrences.

- Assess and rank the quality of internal controls *(H, M, L)* and the reason for the assessment. Internal controls mitigate the inherent risk and involve the implementation of policies, procedures and standards.
- Calculate the residual risk level *(H, M, L)* that remains after considering the relevant internal controls. For example, a medium inherent risk and low-quality internal controls will result in a high residual risk level.

Risk prioritization

By using the results of the RCSA for each business unit, the key risks should be prioritized based on the residual risk levels. All high residual risks should be discussed with the risk-management steering committee, and risk-mitigation plans (RMPs) should be developed.

Risk-mitigation plans

RMPs must be established by taking a risk-based approach to address areas with the greatest control weaknesses and largest potential for loss. Organizations will generally run out of resources before they run out of risk; therefore, high-risk items must be prioritized.

Completion dates should be targeted, and responsible owners are selected to facilitate the risk-mitigation process.

Information and communication

Relevant information is identified, captured and communicated in a form and time frame that enables people to carry out their responsibilities. Information for identifying, assessing and responding to risk is needed at all levels of an entity.

Monitoring

ERM is monitored, and modifications are made as necessary. In this way, the organization can react dynamically, changing as conditions warrant.

Risk monitoring and reporting

The key risks that were identified must be monitored and periodically reported to the senior management and board of directors.

Scenario planning and stress testing

Among the many tools that a manager can use for strategic analysis, scenario planning can capture a wide range of possibilities with specific details. By identifying fundamental trends, the technology executive can define a series of scenarios that will assist the organization in reducing errors in the decision-making process.

"Scenarios are thorough and probable views of how business environments might extend into the future" (Ringland, 2002).

Step 1: Brainstorm future scenarios

In the first step, the time frame is determined based on the following factors:

- The lifecycle of the product.
- Political conditions within the country.
- Competitor analysis.
- Technological advancement.

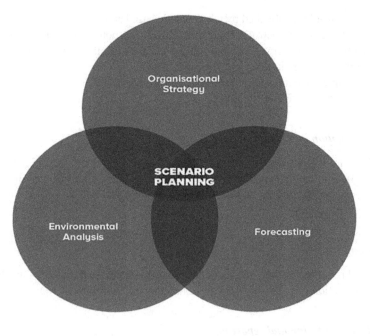

© Copyright KnowledgeBrief

Figure 2.2 The elements of scenario planning (Ringland, 2002).

Step 2: Identify trends and driving forces

Consider the following factors:

- Who has an interest in these decisions?
- Who will be affected by them?
- Who could influence them?

The apparent driving forces include but are not limited to suppliers, customers, competitors, employees, shareholders and government. Identification of the following factors is also essential:

- Current roles of the driving forces.
- Their interests.
- Their positions in the field.
- Their progress over time.

Step 3: Create a scenario planning template

The driving forces of the environment are identified from the key factors identified in Step 2. These driving forces can originate in the following areas:

- Society and its structures, including demographic, economic and political factors, as well as public opinion.
- Markets and customer behaviour.
- Technology and innovation.
- The organization's competitive structure within its industry.
- The organization's organizational capacities and core competencies.

The forces that are highly predictable should be identified so that the organization can focus on the effects that are less likely to occur.

Step 4: Develop a scenario

The essential task of scenario planning is developing the actual scenario. Through this phase, a situation should be built that incorporates each factor evaluated in the earlier steps and considers the traits and trends of the market. In building a scenario, the strengths and weaknesses of the plan should be identified and considered.

Step 5: Evaluate a scenario

Through a systematic step-by-step procedure, the scenario team can achieve a balance between creativity and free-form imagination by using sound judgement based on knowledge and experience.

Scenario analysis

Scenario analysis shows a forward-looking view of operational *risk* that augments historical internal and external data. These exercises allow stakeholders to identify and *manage risk* exposures through business decisions and *risk*-mitigation strategies.

Threat actor analysis: Identify actors who pose a threat to the organization.

Impact analysis: Determine the areas that the organization is focused on protecting.

Scenario selection: Determine scenarios that could have a catastrophic impact on the organization.

At minimum, a scenario should include the following:

The situation: An explanation of the sequence of events that leads to an adverse outcome. These may be industry and organization specific but must include items such as the following:

- Business continuity planning (BCP) events.
- External attacks by hackers, competitors or government agencies.
- Malicious insiders stealing information.
- Accidental release of confidential information.
- The mishandling of data by vendors and third parties.

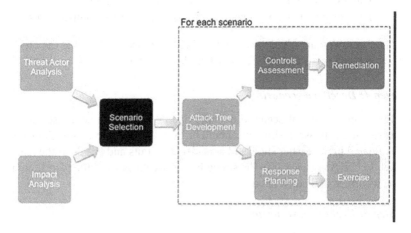

Figure 2.3 The process of scenario analysis.

The outcomes: Outcomes that are unfavourable to an organization and are a result of the event *should be* clearly identified. An event may have multiple outcomes; for example, the same scenario may result in the loss of revenue, legal costs and regulatory fines. Each outcome should be explicitly laid out, and its impact should be described.

Controls in place: Controls work as separate lines of defence, at times sequentially and at other times interacting with each other to help prevent the occurrence of an adverse event. Often, the correct operation of one control may provide adequate protection or mitigation. If controls operate independently of each other, as they often do, the combined probability of all of them failing simultaneously tends to be significantly lower than the probability of any one of them failing.

Frequency of occurrence: The frequency or likelihood of the scenario being realized should be a part of the scenario analysis and is best estimated in a discussion with management.

Severity of the outcomes: The severity of each of the adverse outcomes should be estimated separately.

Scenario examples are as follows:

- Scenario #1: Patch management.
- Scenario #2: Network ransomware/malware attack.
- Scenario #3: Unplanned attack.
- Scenario #4: Financial break-in/external attack.
- Scenario #5: Cloud security breach.

Attack tree development: Develop detailed attack trees for each scenario.

Control assessment: Map controls to the attack tree and assess effectiveness.

Remediation: Use the control assessment to plan remediation projects that address control gaps.

Response planning: Create or enhance existing response plans to cater to extreme scenarios.

Exercise: Test the control strength, response plan and overall preparedness.

Step 6: Update strategies and policies accordingly

One or two months after the scenarios are implemented, it is essential to evaluate the strategic plan and update the policies. This evaluation and update process should be completed on a periodic basis.

3 Alignment with enterprise risk management

Operational risk management

Operational risk is defined by the Bank of International Settlements (BIS) as "the risk of loss resulting from inadequate or failed internal processes, people and systems or from external events (strategic and reputational risk is not included in this definition for the purpose of a minimum regulatory operational risk capital charge)" (Basel Committee on Banking Supervision, 2001).

Legal risk is included in this definition. Operational risk is therefore the sum of operating, information systems, compliance and legal risk.

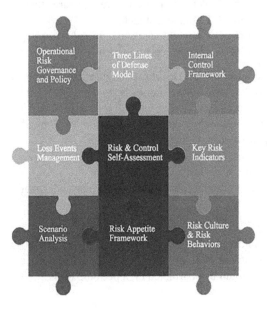

Figure 3.1 The elements of operational risk management through the Sergio Galanti operational risk puzzle (Caldas, 2006).

DOI: 10.4324/9781003200895-3

In addition to the responsibility to protect organizational assets from the threats that exist in the current environment, risk managers must consider and manage risks to individuals when information systems process sensitive information—that is, personally identifiable information (PII).

Information security aspects of operational risk

Security risk management provides a means of better understanding the nature of security threats and their interaction at an individual, organizational, or community level (Standards Australia, 2006, p. 6). Generically, the risk-management process can be applied to the security risk management context. The risk-management process advocated in ISO 31000 should be used as the foundation for risk management in an organization; however, security risk management has several unique processes that other forms of risk management do not consider.

The core of security risk management is identical to ERM, which has been discussed in Chapter 2, with the addition of informational assessments, such as threats, criticality registers and vulnerability assessments. Security risk management is the integration between risk management and these assessment forms.

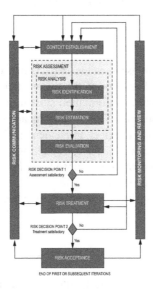

Figure 3.2 The Information Technology – Security Techniques – Information Security Risk-Management process (ISO, 2020).

Cybersecurity risk-assessment process

Information security risk management is the systematic application of management policies, procedures and practices to establish the context for information security risks and for identifying, analysing, evaluating, treating, monitoring and communicating those risks.

ISO 27005 is the "Information Technology – Security Techniques – Information Security Risk Management" standard released by the International Organization for Standardization (ISO) to provide guidance for the information security risk-management processes that are needed to implement an effective information security management system (ISMS). Although this standard is considered a risk-management standard, a significant portion addresses information security risk assessments, which are a key part of a risk-management programme.

ISO 27005 is aligned with NIST SP 800–30 and is written from a high-level perspective compared to other frameworks. ISO 27005 has five major topic areas:

i   Information security risk assessment.
ii   Information security risk treatment.
iii Information security risk acceptance.
iv   Information security risk communication.
v   Information security risk monitoring and review.

Risk identification

Information security risk assesses the impacts that can occur on an organization and its stakeholders due to the threats and vulnerabilities associated with the operation of its information systems and the environments in which those systems operate. The primary means of mitigating information security-related risk is to select, implement, maintain and continuously monitor preventative, detective and corrective security controls to protect information assets from compromise or to limit the damage to an organization should a compromise occur.

Risk identification consists of five main activities that are discussed in the following sections.

Identification of assets

The objective of this activity is to identify the assets that are in the scope of the risk assessment, including the asset owners. In ISO 27005, assets are categorized as either primary or secondary. Primary assets are core processes, activities and information and secondary assets are hardware, software, network, personnel, site and structure.

Identification of threats

The objective of this step is to prepare a list of potential threats to each asset. According to ISO 27005, stakeholders such as asset owners, users, human resources staff and facilities management can assist in identifying these threats. ISO 27005 also states that internal experience, particularly based on previous incidents or assessments, should be considered. One of the most useful contributions of ISO 27005 is the inclusion of standardized threat catalogues.

Identification of existing controls

The objective of this activity is to identify existing controls. The guidance provided within ISO 27005 for this activity is open ended and does not specifically address the criteria or scale of the control review. ISO 27005 does provide references to information sources that may be able to assist in this activity. Examples of information sources for this part of the review are as follows:

- Documents that have information about controls.
- People responsible for information security.
- Onsite reviews.
- Review of internal audit results.

Identification of vulnerabilities

The goal is to identify an asset's vulnerabilities through the following actions:

- Vulnerability scanning and penetration testing.
- Code reviews.
- Interviews.
- Questionnaires.
- Physical inspection.
- Document analysis.

Identification of consequences

The objective of this activity is to determine the possible damage or consequences that could be caused by an "incident scenario" or what other frameworks refer to as a threat scenario. ISO 27005 provides a list of impact factors that can be used to identify and measure consequences.

Expressing and measuring risk

Information security risk "is measured in terms of a combination of the likelihood of an event and its consequence".

It is further defined as an information security event, meaning "an identified occurrence of a system, service or network state indicating a possible breach of information security policy or failure of safeguards, or a previously unknown situation that may be security relevant".

In measuring risk, it is not the risk of a single, critical event that matters but the general map of risk composed of all possible critical events. This enables the assessor to determine the total risk, especially of probable events or especially severe events. There are two fundamental areas of risk that allow possible critical events to be classified during analysis according to their importance for the appropriate functioning of the organization. The first is operational security, and the second is business continuity.

Risk analysis

Risk analysis consists of determining and evaluating the following:

* Processes that enable the realization of organizational tasks.
* Disruptive phenomena and the probability of their occurrence.
* Resource vulnerability in the sense of the magnitude of disruptive phenomena and their potential influence on organizational activity.

Risk analysis is a prerequisite for subsequently treating risk. Risk treatment pertains to controlling the risk so that it remains within acceptable levels. Risk can be reduced by applying security measures.

Risk can also be

* shared by outsourcing or insuring,
* avoided and
* accepted, in the sense that the organization accepts the likely impact of a security incident.

The likelihood of a security incident occurring is a function of the likelihood that a threat will appear and that the threat will be able to successfully exploit the relevant system vulnerabilities. The consequences of the occurrence of a security incident are a function of the likely impact the incident will have on the organization as a result of the harm sustained by the organization's assets.

Risk evaluation and quantification

Risk evaluation is the process of comparing the results of the risk analysis with the risk evaluation criteria defined to determine whether the cyber-risks are acceptable. The following are the basic steps of the risk evaluation process:

- Identification.
- Probability and impact.
- Identified risk.
- Treatment.
- Secondary risk.
- Residual risk.
- Monitoring and review.

Organization-wide security and privacy risk should be assessed, and the risk-assessment results should be updated on an ongoing basis. There are two types of risk assessment:

- Qualitative.
- Quantitative.

Risk-mitigation planning and verification

Risk-mitigation planning is the process of developing options and actions to enhance opportunities and reduce threats to project objectives. Risk-mitigation implementation is the process of executing risk-mitigation actions. Risk-mitigation progress monitoring includes tracking identified risks, identifying new risks and evaluating risk process effectiveness throughout the initiative.

The risk-mitigation step involves the development of mitigation plans designed to manage, eliminate or reduce risk to an acceptable level. Once a plan is implemented, it is continually monitored to assess its efficacy with the intent of revising the course of action if needed.

General guidelines for applying risk-mitigation management options are based on the assessed combination of the probability of occurrence and the severity of the consequences of an identified risk.

Risk treatment

Risk modification

The introduction of an additional factor that can positively or negatively influence risk.

Risk transfer

The identification of ways and means to transfer a risk, either through the acquisition of insurance (i.e., cyber insurance) or by outsourcing.

Risk avoidance

Electing not to pursue a business activity that would cause the risk to appear.

Risk acceptance

Conscious and deliberate acceptance of the identified level of risk, without any other alteration by way of modification or transference.

Risk remediation

The selection of a range of tactics, techniques and procedures to reduce an asset's susceptibility to compromise.

Risk communication

Risk communication is an important tool for disseminating information and improving the understanding of risk-management decisions. This understanding and information enable stakeholders to make informed decisions about how the decision will impact their interests and values.

Risk monitoring and review

Risk monitoring and review is the process of identifying, analysing and planning for newly discovered risks and managing identified risks. Throughout the process, the risk owners track identified risks, reveal new risks, implement risk response plans and gauge the effectiveness of risk response plans.

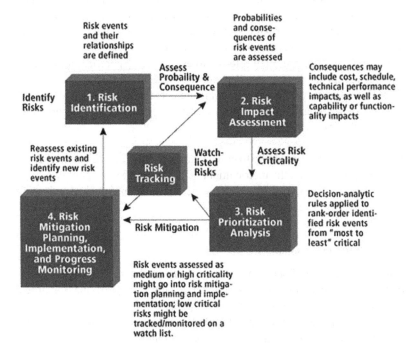

Figure 3.3 The foundational risk-management process (The MITRE Institute, 2007).

Loss event management

Understanding and managing loss events are essential to an effective operational risk-management programme. This process includes the frequency, amount, type and source of loss events as well as a comprehensive list of loss events.

Security metrics

Metrics can provide insights into information security programme effectiveness, levels of regulatory compliance, and the ability of staff and departments to address security issues for which they are responsible. Metrics can also help identify levels of risk in not taking certain mitigation actions and thus provide guidance for prioritizing future resource investments. Because metrics provide concrete facts and a common vocabulary for communicating risks, they may additionally be used to raise the level of security awareness within the organization.

Security metrics are tools designed to facilitate decision-making and improve performance and accountability by collecting, analysing and reporting relevant performance-related data. IT security metrics are based on IT security performance goals and objectives.

Effective metrics are often referred to as SMART (specific, measurable, attainable, repeatable and time dependent). These metrics should also indicate the degree to which security goals are achieved and facilitate actions to improve the organization's overall security programme. It is important to consider the following:

- How difficult it might be to collect accurate data for a given metric.
- The potential that the metric might be misinterpreted.
- The need to periodically review metrics that are being tracked and make changes as needed.

Key performance indicators

A KPI is a measure of performance commonly used to help an organization define and evaluate how successful it is, typically in terms of making progress towards its long-term organizational goals.

The following are some examples of clear cybersecurity metrics that can be tracked and easily presented to relevant stakeholders.

Level of preparedness: How many devices on an organization's network are fully patched and up to date?

Unidentified devices on the internal network: How many such devices are on an organization's network?

Intrusion attempts: How many times have attackers breached the organization's network?

Mean time to detect (MTTD): How long do security threats go unnoticed? MTTD measures how long it takes for an organization to become aware of a potential security incident.

Mean time to resolve (MTTR): How long does it take an organization to respond to a threat once it has been uncovered?

Days to patch: How long does it take an organization to implement security patches?

Cybersecurity awareness training results: Who has taken (and completed) training? Did they understand the material?

Number of cybersecurity incidents reported: Are users reporting cybersecurity issues to the organization?

Security ratings: Often, the easiest way to communicate metrics to non-technical colleagues is through an easy-to-understand scorecard.

Key risk indicators

A key risk indicator (KRI) is a measure used by management to indicate the risk associated with an activity. KRIs are metrics used by an organization to provide early signals of increasing risk exposure in various areas of the enterprise.

KRI examples

- Information security training completeness.
- Policy exceptions/deviations.
- Phishing campaign failure rate.
- Outstanding audit findings.
- Risk-assessment ratings.
- Patch coverage by system.
- Incidents and events.
- Breaches.
- Vulnerabilities by criticality and age.
- Account management.

Risk culture and risk behaviours

Risk culture is the system of values and behaviours present in an organization that shapes the risk decisions of management and employees. One element of risk culture is a common understanding of the organization and its business purpose.

The risk culture of an organization is likely to

- determine the degree to which the organization's policies are internalized by staff and exhibited in day-to-day behaviour,
- determine staff response to threats or situations that fall outside well-prescribed operating guidelines and
- influence the organization's reputation among regulators, clients and the broader market.

4 Risk-management practice – vulnerability management

Patch and vulnerability management is a security management practice designed to proactively prevent the exploitation of IT vulnerabilities that exist within enterprise systems. The expected result is the reduction of time and finances spent by an organization when handling the impact of unintentional/intentional attacks on an organization—that is, malware/ransomware. Proactively managing the vulnerabilities within systems will either reduce or eliminate the potential for exploitation. Integrating this programme within risk-management practices provides executive management teams with a focus on the appropriate level of risk assumed by their organization when existing vulnerabilities are properly monitored.

Figure 4.1 The elements of the vulnerability management process (Huntsman, 2017).

DOI: 10.4324/9781003200895-4

Patches are additional pieces of code developed to address problems commonly known as bugs in software. They enable additional functionality or address security flaws within a programme. Vulnerabilities are flaws that can be exploited by a malicious entity to gain greater access or privileges than it is authorized to have on a computer system. Not all vulnerabilities have related patches; therefore, system administrators must be aware not only of applicable vulnerabilities and available patches but also of other methods of remediation—that is, device or network configuration changes and employee training that limits the exposure of systems to vulnerabilities.

An organization should implement a vulnerability management programme to address its information security vulnerabilities through a comprehensive and continuous process of identifying, classifying, remediating and mitigating vulnerabilities.

Maintain an asset inventory

Stakeholders within an organization should maintain an asset inventory of IT resources to determine the type of hardware, operating system (OS) and software applications in use. In addition, stakeholders should maintain an inventory of IT assets that is updated regularly as part of the system configuration management process. An organization is responsible for determining the purpose and use of the inventory and maintains only the information needed for those uses. The resources within the inventory should be grouped and assigned priority levels to facilitate remediation efforts and may include the following:

1   Associated system name.
2   Property number.
3   Owner of the IT resource—that is, the main user.
4   System administrator.
5   Physical location.
6   Connected network port.
7   Software configuration.

    a   OS and version number.
    b   Software packages and version numbers.
    c   Network services.
    d   IP address (if static).

8   Hardware configuration.

    a   Central processing unit.
    b   Memory.
    c   Disk space.

    d   Ethernet addresses—that is, network cards.
    e   Wireless capability.
    f   Input/output capability—that is, Universal Serial Bus, Firewire.

9   Firmware versions.

Prioritize assets

An organization should define the risk and critical value for each device within the asset inventory. It is important to identify the importance of the device and the individual(s) responsible for approving access to it.

The following factors are important in understanding the strategic factors and gaining a clear understanding of details:

- Risk appetite.
- Risk tolerance level.
- Risk-mitigation practices and policies for each device.
- Residual risk treatment.
- Countermeasures for each device or service (if a service is correlated with the device).
- Business impact analysis.

Assess vulnerabilities

The following sections describe the methods utilized to effectively complete a vulnerability assessment process using any automated or manual tool.

System baseline definition

Information about the system is gathered before the vulnerability assessment, and the following information is reviewed:

- Whether the device has the appropriate open ports, processes and services.
- The approved drivers and software that should be installed on the device.
- The basic configuration of each device; for example, if the device is a perimeter device, it should not be configured to contain a default administrator username.

Vulnerability scan

Vulnerability scanners are commonly used in many organizations to identify vulnerabilities on hosts and networks. A vulnerability scanner identifies not only hosts and open ports on those hosts but also the associated vulnerabilities. A host OS and active applications are identified and then compared with a database of known vulnerabilities.

Vulnerability scanners can be of two types.

Network scanners are used to map an organization's network and identify open ports, vulnerable software and misconfigured services. They can be installed on a single system on the network and can quickly locate and test numerous hosts.

Network scanners are generally ineffective at gathering accurate information on hosts using personal firewalls unless personal firewalls are configured to permit network scanning activity.

Host scanners must be installed on each host to be tested. These scanners are used primarily to identify specific host OS and application misconfigurations and vulnerabilities. Host scanners have high detection granularity and usually require not only host (local) access but also a root or administrative account. Some host scanners offer the capability of repairing misconfigurations.

An organization's vulnerability scanners provide the following capabilities:

- Identify active hosts on networks.
- Identify active and vulnerable services (ports) on hosts.
- Identify vulnerabilities associated with the discovered OSs and applications.
- Test compliance with host application usage/security policies.
- Identify out-of-date software versions and applicable patches or system upgrades.

Prior to starting a vulnerability scan, an organization's technology group should integrate the applicable compliance requirements into the configuration. The recommended approach includes the use of related tools and plug-ins on the platform being assessed:

- Best scan—that is, popular ports.
- CMS web scans—that is, Joomla, WordPress, Drupal, general CMS.
- Quick scan.
- Most common ports best scan—that is, 65,535 ports.
- Firewall scan.
- Stealth scan.

Aggressive scan

- Full scan, identifying exploitation and distributed denial-of-service (DDoS) attacks.

- Open Web Application Security Project (OWASP) Top 10 Scan and OWASP checks.
- PCI DSS preparation for web applications.
- Health Insurance Portability and Accountability Act (HIPAA) policy scan for compliance.

Vulnerability assessment report

The vulnerability assessment report should include the following:

- Risk-mitigation techniques based on the criticality of the assets and results.
- Findings related to any possible gap between the results and the system baseline definition—that is, deviations in any misconfiguration and discoveries made.
- Recommendations to correct the deviations and mitigate possible vulnerabilities.

High and medium vulnerabilities should be detailed within the report to include the following:

- The name of the vulnerability.
- The date of discovery.
- The score based on common vulnerabilities and exposures (CVE) databases.
- A detailed description of the vulnerability.
- Details of the affected systems and the process for correcting the vulnerability.
- A proof of concept (PoC) of the vulnerability for the system, if possible.
- A blank field for the owner of the vulnerability, the time it took to correct the vulnerability, the next revision and countermeasures between the identification of the vulnerability and the final solution.

Prioritize vulnerability remediation

Stakeholders should prioritize the order in which the organization addresses vulnerability remediation. The technology organization is responsible for monitoring security sources for vulnerability announcements, patch and non-patch remediations and threats that correspond to the software within the organizational inventory. A variety of sources should be monitored to ensure that the appropriate stakeholders are aware of all newly discovered vulnerabilities.

Types of security concerns

The technology organization is responsible for monitoring vulnerabilities, remediations and threats:

- *Vulnerabilities* are software flaws or misconfigurations that cause a weakness in the security of a system and can be exploited by a malicious entity to violate policies.
- *Remediations* include three primary methods:
  - Installation of a software patch.
  - Adjustment of a configuration setting.
  - Removal of the affected software.

- *Threats* are capabilities or methods of attack developed by malicious entities to exploit vulnerabilities and potentially cause harm to a computer system or network. Threats usually take the form of exploit scripts, worms, viruses, rootkits and Trojan horses.

System administrators should monitor systems under their control running software that is not contained in the organizational inventory for vulnerabilities, remediations and threats.

Monitor vulnerabilities, remediations and threats

There are several types of resources available for monitoring the status of vulnerabilities, remediations and threats. Each type of resource has its own strengths and weaknesses.

It is recommended that more than one type of resource be used to ensure accurate and timely knowledge. The most common types of resources are as follows:

- Vendor websites and mailing lists.
- Third-party websites.
- Third-party mailing lists and newsgroups.
- Vulnerability scanners.
- Vulnerability databases.
- Enterprise patch management tools.

An organization can monitor vulnerabilities, remediation and threats using the following resource types:

- Enterprise patch management tool to obtain all available patches from supported vendors.
- Vendor security mailing lists and websites to obtain all available patches from vendors not supported by the enterprise patch management tool.

- The vulnerability database is the National Vulnerability Database or mailing list to obtain immediate information on all known vulnerabilities and suggested remediations.
- Third-party vulnerability mailing lists—that is, the US-CERT Cybersecurity Alerts that highlight the most critical vulnerabilities.

After the initial assessment of a new vulnerability, remediation or threat, the technology team should continue to monitor updates and new information.

Prioritize vulnerability remediation

The technology group should consider each threat and its potential impact on the organization when setting priorities for vulnerability remediation.
   This evaluation includes the following:

- Determine the significance of the threat or vulnerability.
- Establish which systems are vulnerable or exposed, with a focus on systems that are essential for the operation and other high-priority systems.
- Evaluate the impact on the systems, organization and network if the vulnerability is not removed and is exploited.
- Determine the existence, extent and spread of related worms, viruses or exploitation.
- Ascertain whether malicious code has been published and the level of distribution.
- Determine the damage caused, such as system access, information disclosure, arbitrary code execution or denial of service.
- Determine the risks involved in applying patch or non-patch remediation.
- Identify whether the remediation will affect the functionality of other software applications or services through research and testing.
- Establish what degree of risk is acceptable.

Maintain a specific remediation database

The technology group should maintain a database of remediations to be applied within the organization. Enterprise patch management tools usually supply a relevant database. The technology group may also manually maintain a separate database of IT technologies that are not supported by the patch management tool.

Conduct generic testing of remediations

The technology group should test patches and non-patch remediations on IT devices that use standardized configurations. System administrators are responsible for testing patches and non-patch remediations to mitigate vulnerabilities and threats identified for software that is not monitored by the technology group. Remediation testing guidelines may include the following:

- Most vendors provide some type of authentication mechanism. A downloaded patch should be checked against any of the authenticity methods provided by the vendor, including cryptographic checksums, signatures and digital certificates.
- A virus scan should also run on all patches before installation. Before running the scan, the system administrator should ensure that the virus signature database in the anti-virus programme is up to date.
- Patches and configuration modifications should be tested on non-production systems since remediation can easily produce unintended consequences.
- Installing one patch might also inadvertently uninstall or disable another patch. If there is a dependency, it is important to ensure that patches are installed in the correct sequence.
- Testing should be performed on a selection of systems that accurately represent the configuration of the systems in deployment, since so many possible system configurations exist that a vendor cannot possibly test all of them.

Deploy vulnerability remediations

An organization should deploy vulnerability remediations to applicable systems, to include those that are not at immediate risk of exploitation. Vulnerability remediation should also be incorporated into the organization's standard builds and configurations for hosts.

There are three primary methods of remediation that can be applied to an affected system.

Security patch installation

- Applying a security patch, also called a fix or hotfix, repairs the vulnerability since patches contain code that modifies the software application to address and eliminate the problem.
- Patches downloaded from vendor websites are typically the most up to date and are usually free of malicious codes.

Configuration adjustment

- Adjusting how an application or security control is configured can effectively block attack vectors and reduce the threat of exploitation. Common configuration adjustments include disabling services and modifying privileges as well as changing firewall rules and modifying router access controls.

- Settings of vulnerable software applications can be modified by adjusting file attributes or registry settings.

Software removal

- Removing or uninstalling the affected software or vulnerable service eliminates vulnerability and any associated threat. This is a practical solution when an application is not needed on a system.
- Determining how the system is used, removing unnecessary software and services, and running only what is essential for the system's purpose are recommended security practices.

Prior to installing a patch, administrators should ensure that a current full backup of the system being patched is maintained. Regardless of whether remediation involves automated patching or manual updates, system administrators may believe that the disadvantages of a suggested remediation outweigh its benefits. They may not wish to install the patches or perform configuration modifications. The reasons behind these decisions should be documented and communicated to the technology team and then to the appropriate management for approval.

Assess risk

The risk of delaying remediation must be weighed carefully. Risk assessments that determine the amount of risk to the network are another way to help determine the state of vulnerability management within the enterprise.

Technology groups can use risk-assessment information to determine which assets should be patched first or whether any systems can afford to absorb the risk associated with them. However, it is difficult to rate the risk of a new vulnerability without knowing how this risk will affect the network-connected assets.

When assessing the risk, the technology team should consider the issues discussed in the following sections.

Threat level

Do(es) the system(s) that require remediation face numerous and/or significant threats? For example, public web servers and most federal government organizations may face high threat levels.

Risk of compromise

What is the likelihood that a compromise will occur? If the vulnerability is easy to exploit, then remediation should be applied swiftly.

Consequences of compromise

What are the consequences of compromise? If the system is critical or contains sensitive data, then remediation should be performed immediately.

This holds true even for non-critical systems if a successful exploitation would lead to an attacker gaining full control of the system.

*Distribute vulnerability and remediation information
to local administrators*

The technology team is responsible for informing local administrators about vulnerabilities and remediations that correspond to software packages within the team's scope that are in the organizational software inventory.

Patch management

Widespread manual patching of computers is ineffective, as the number of patches that need to be installed is significant, and it is impractical for individuals to keep systems up to date with this method. While patching and vulnerability monitoring can often appear to be an overwhelming task, consistent mitigation of organizational vulnerabilities can be achieved through a tested and integrated patching process that makes efficient use of automated patching technology. Enterprise patch management tools allow the technology team or a group that it works closely with to automatically and quickly push patches out to many computers.

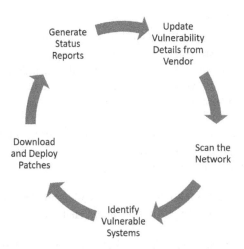

Figure 4.2 The patch management lifecycle (ManageEngine, 2020).

Deploy enterprise patch management tools using a phased approach

Implementing patch management tools in phases allows process and user communication issues to be addressed with a small group before deploying the patch application consistently. Most organizations deploy patch management tools first to standardized desktop systems and single-platform server farms of similarly configured servers. Once this has been accomplished, organizations should address the more difficult issue of integrating multi-platform environments, non-standard desktop systems, legacy computers and computers with unusual configurations. It may be necessary to use manual methods for OSs and applications not supported by automated patching tools as well as some computers with unusual configurations. For these types of systems, there should be a written and implemented procedure for the manual patching process and the technology group should coordinate local administrator efforts.

Perform automated deployment of patches

The technology group should automatically deploy patches to IT devices using enterprise patch management tools. Once a patch management technology has been selected, an organization's IT administrators are responsible for designing a solution architecture, performing testing, deploying and securing the solution and maintaining operations and security.

Technology security

Deploying enterprise patch management tools within an enterprise strengthens the security posture in an organization through vulnerability reduction. These tools usually increase security specifically when they contain built-in security measures to protect against security risks and threats. The following are some risks associated with using these tools:

- A patch may have been altered (inadvertently or intentionally).
- Credentials may be misused.
- Vulnerabilities in the solution components (including agents) may be exploited.
- An entity could monitor tool communications to identify vulnerabilities (particularly when the host is on an external network).

The organization can reduce these risks by applying standard security techniques that should be used when deploying any enterprise-wide application.

Examples of countermeasures include the following:

- Keep the patching solution components tightly secured, including patching them.
- Encrypt network communications.
- Verify the integrity of patches before installing them—that is, use checksums.
- Test patches before deployment to identify corruption.

Patch management process

The fundamental considerations that an organization should integrate into its patch management process are discussed in the following sections.

Discovery

The technology group ensures that the organization has a comprehensive, accurate network inventory that includes the following:

- Understanding the types of devices.
- OSs.
- OS versions.
- Third-party applications.

Standardization and categorization

The technology group should implement a standardized approach to ensure, when possible, that devices run the same OS, use the same hardware, are configured in the same manner and run the same applications. The technology group should segment managed systems and/or users according to risk and priority based on the following aspects:

- Machine types—that is, server, laptop, etc.
- OSs.
- OS versions.
- User roles.

Patch management policy creation

The technology group should create patching criteria by establishing what will be patched, when, and under what conditions. For example, the following should be considered:

- The frequency of the patching cycle—that is, the patching schedule for laptop end users may be weekly, while patching for servers may be less frequent and more manual.
- The patching rollout cycle—that is, browser updates versus OS updates, critical versus non-critical updates.
- Identification of maintenance windows to avoid disruption—that is, consider time zones for "follow the sun" patching.
- Creation of exceptions.

Monitor new patches and vulnerabilities

The technology group should implement a process to effectively:

- understand vendor patch release schedules and models and identify reliable sources for timely vulnerability disclosures and
- create a process for evaluating emergency patches.

Patch testing

The technology group should ensure that an appropriate test environment is in place to

- test that patches are working appropriately before production deployment,
- create backups for easy rollback if necessary,
- validate successful deployment and
- monitor incompatibility or performance issues.

Configuration management

The technology group should have a mechanism in to place to capture any changes made throughout the patching process.

Patch deployment

Patch deployment should be well documented, with a planned outline for the changes that will occur once the patch is applied. The technology group should have an automated patch management process that facilitates scheduled regular update scans and ensures that patches are applied during non-peak periods. Clear fallback policies should be in place for patch deployment issues.

Patch auditing

The technology group should have a patch audit process in place to identify any failed or pending patches, including continuous monitoring for any unexpected incompatibility or performance issues.

Reporting

The technology group should have a mechanism in place to produce a patch compliance report when required. This includes documenting risk acceptance and any exceptions that may occur.

Review, improve and repeat

The technology group should have an established cadence for repeating and optimizing the patch management process, including the following:

* Phasing out or isolating any outdated or unsupported machines.
* Reviewing applicable policies.
* Revisiting exceptions to verify whether they still apply or are necessary.

Verify vulnerability remediation through network and host vulnerability scanning

The technology group and system administrators should verify that they have successfully remediated or mitigated vulnerabilities as intended.

The technology group should confirm that the remediations have been conducted appropriately to avoid a security incident or unplanned downtime. This can be accomplished by several methods:

* Verify that the files or configuration settings that the remediation was intended to correct have been changed as stated in the vendor's documentation.
* Scan the host with a vulnerability scanner to detect known vulnerabilities.
* Review patch logs to verify that the recommended patches were installed properly.
* Employ exploitation procedures or code to attempt to exploit the vulnerability—that is, perform a penetration test.

Generally, exploitation tests involve launching actual attacks within a network or on a host, and this type of testing should be performed only on non-production equipment for certain vulnerabilities.

Review the patch log

Log files keep track of the history of a system. Patch logs can assist the technology group, as well as system administrators, with tracking and verifying installed patches. Using patch logs to monitor an organization's systems helps achieve consistency and compliance with the remediation plan.

An organization's patch logs provide the following capabilities:

*   Identify which patches are installed on a system, allowing easy confirmation that the appropriate set of patches has been applied.
*   Ensure that patches are applied consistently across the organization through a comparison of log files.
*   Verify that a patch has been installed properly.
*   Determine whether the patch or a subsequent update improperly removed or damaged a previous patch.

Check patch levels

An organization should consider verifying the patch levels of hosts. In most deployments, each host runs an agent that monitors various characteristics, such as OSs and application patches and anti-virus updates. When the host attempts to connect to the network, a network device such as a router requests information from the host's agent. If the host does not respond to the request or the response indicates that the host is not fully patched, the network device causes the host to be placed on a separate virtual local area network (VLAN). This allows the organization to update the unpatched hosts while severely restricting functionality. Once a host on the VLAN has been fully updated, it is moved automatically from the VLAN to the organization's regular network. The VLAN strategy can be particularly helpful for ensuring that mobile hosts are fully patched.

Vulnerability remediation training

An organization should train administrators in how to apply vulnerability remediations. In organizations that rely on end users to patch computers, the technology group must also train users in this function.

Deploy security metrics

This section discusses the development of patch and vulnerability metrics in the context of measuring characteristics per system. The word "system" here refers to a set of IT assets, processes, applications and related resources that are under the same direct management and budgetary control and have the same function or mission objective, have essentially the same security needs and reside in the same general operating environment.

Type of patch and vulnerability metrics

There are three main categories of patch and vulnerability metrics:

* Susceptibility to attack.
* Mitigation response time.
* Cost.

An organization's susceptibility to attack can be approximated by several measurements. An organization can measure the following:

* Number of patches needed.
* Number of vulnerabilities.
* Number of network services running on a per-system basis.

These measurements should be taken individually for each computer within the system, and the results should then be aggregated to determine the system-wide results. Both raw results and ratios—that is, the number of vulnerabilities per computer—are important. The raw results help reveal the overall risk that a system faces because the more vulnerabilities, unapplied patches and exposed network services exist, the greater the chance that the system will be penetrated. Large systems consisting of many computers are thus inherently less secure than smaller similarly configured systems.

The organization should consider using ratios when comparing the effectiveness of the security programmes of multiple systems. Ratios allow effective comparisons between systems. Both raw results and ratios should be measured and published for each system, as appropriate, since both are useful and serve different purposes. The initial measurement approach should not consider system security perimeter architectures—that is, firewalls that would prevent an attacker from directly accessing vulnerabilities on system computers. The default position should be to secure all computers within a system even if the system is protected by a strong security perimeter.

Because most systems will not be fully secured, for a variety of reasons, the measurement should then be recalculated while factoring in the system's security perimeter architecture. This will provide a meaningful measurement of a system's actual susceptibility to external attackers. For example, this second measurement should not count vulnerabilities, network services or needed patches on a computer if they cannot be exploited through the system's main firewall.

While the initial measurement of a system's susceptibility to attack should not consider the system security perimeter architecture, it may be desirable to consider an individual computer's security architecture. For example, vulnerabilities exploitable by network connections might not be counted if a computer's personal firewall would prevent such exploitation attempts.

Number of patches

It is natural for organizations that have deployed enterprise patch management tools to measure the number of patches needed per system since these tools automatically provide such data. The number of patches needed is of some value in approximating an organization's susceptibility to attack, but the effectiveness of this measurement is limited because a particular security patch may fix one or many vulnerabilities, and these vulnerabilities may be of varying levels of severity. In addition, vulnerabilities for which there are no patches are often published. These vulnerabilities intensify the risk to organizations but cannot be captured by measuring the number of patches needed. The quality of this measurement can be improved by factoring in the number of patches rated critical by the issuing vendor and comparing the number of critical and non-critical patches.

Number of vulnerabilities

The number of vulnerabilities that exist per system is a better measure of an organization's susceptibility to attack. This metric would be included as a reporting output from the organization's vulnerability scanning tools. As with measuring patches, the organization should consider the severity ratings of the vulnerabilities and group the number of vulnerabilities at each severity level or range of severity levels. The true impact of each vulnerability can be determined only by reviewing it in the context of the organizational environment. In addition, the impact of a vulnerability on a system depends on the network location of the system; that is, when the system is accessible from the Internet, vulnerabilities are usually more serious.

Number of network services running on a per-system basis

The concept behind this metric is that each network service represents a potential set of vulnerabilities, so there is an enhanced security risk when systems run additional network services.

On a large system, this measurement can indicate susceptibility to network attacks, both current and future. It is also useful to compare the number of network services running between multiple systems to identify systems that are doing a better job at minimizing their network services.

Measuring the effectiveness of patch and vulnerability management

Patch and vulnerability metrics fall into three categories: susceptibility to attack, mitigation response time and cost, including a metric for the business impact of programme failures. The emphasis on patch and vulnerability metrics for a system or IT security programme should reflect the patch and vulnerability management maturity level. For example, attack susceptibility metrics such as the number of patches, vulnerabilities and network services per system are generally more useful for a programme with a low maturity level than for one with a high maturity level. Organizations should document what metrics will be used for each system and the details of each of those metrics. Realistic performance targets for each metric should be communicated to system owners and system security officers. Once these targets have been achieved, more ambitious targets can be set. It is important to carefully raise the bar for patch and vulnerability security to avoid overwhelming system security officers and system administrators.

Mitigation response time

It is also important to measure how quickly an organization can identify, classify and respond to a new vulnerability and mitigate the potential impact. There are three primary response time measurements:

* Vulnerability and patch identification.
* Patch application.
* Emergency security configuration changes.

Response time for vulnerability and patch identification

This metric measures how long it takes the technology group to learn about a new vulnerability or patch. The timing should begin from the moment the vulnerability or patch is officially announced. This measurement should be made for a sampling of different patches and vulnerabilities and should include the various resources utilized by the technology group to gather information.

Response time for patch application

This metric measures how long it takes to apply a patch to all relevant IT devices within the system. The timing should begin from the moment the technology group becomes aware of the patch. This measurement should be made where it is relatively easy for the technology group to verify patch installation.

This measurement should include the individual and aggregate time spent on the following activities:

- Patch analysis.
- Patch testing.
- Configuration management process.
- Patch deployment effort.

Verification can be performed using enterprise patch management tools or through vulnerability scanning, both host and network based. It may be useful to make this measurement on both critical and non-critical security patches.

Response time for emergency configuration changes

This metric applies in situations where a vulnerability exists that must be mitigated but where there is no patch. In such cases, an organization should utilize the change management process that enables emergency configuration changes. The metric should measure the time it takes from the moment the technology group learns about the vulnerability to the moment when an acceptable workaround has been applied and verified. The following list contains examples of emergency processes that can be timed:

- Firewall or router configuration changes.
- Network disconnection.
- Intrusion prevention device activation or reconfiguration.
- E-mail filtering rule addition.
- Computer isolation.
- Emergency notification of staff.

Targeting metrics towards programme maturity

The emphasis on patch and vulnerability metrics for a system or IT security programme should reflect the patch and vulnerability management maturity level. A programme with a low maturity level is likely to have a system with high susceptibility to attack, and metrics such as the vulnerability ratio should be of the highest priority. More mature programmes regularly fix all vulnerabilities; therefore, attack susceptibility metrics are less useful. These programmes should focus on metrics related to their response time to emerging threats and vulnerabilities and optimizing costs.

While it is true that all metrics are important for programmes at all maturity levels, this discussion is intended to prioritize the implementation of metrics.

NIST SP 800–26, Security Self-Assessment Guide for Information Technology Systems, defines maturity levels for various aspects of an IT security programme:

- Level 1 – Control objectives have been documented in a security policy.
- Level 2 – Security controls have been documented as procedures.
- Level 3 – Procedures have been implemented.
- Level 4 – Procedures and security controls have been tested and reviewed.
- Level 5 – Procedures and security controls have been fully integrated into a comprehensive programme.

Patch and vulnerability metrics table

The patch and vulnerability metrics table should be analysed on a per-system basis (Table 4.1).

Table 4.1 The metrics for patch and vulnerability management.

Metrics Name	Unit	Target Maturity Level (NIST)
Vulnerability ratio	Vulnerability/host	3
Unapplied patch ratio	Patches/host	3
Network services ratio	Network services/host	3
Response time for vulnerability and patch identification	Time	4
Patch response time (critical)	Time	4
Patch response time (non-critical)	Time	4
Emergency configuration response time	Time	4

5 Risk-management practice – system development lifecycle

Figure 5.1 Elements of the system development lifecycle (SmartSheet, 2020).

Secure system development lifecycle

A secure system development lifecycle (SDLC) process ensures that security assurance activities, such as penetration testing, code review and architecture

DOI: 10.4324/9781003200895-5

analysis, are an integral part of the development effort. Activities within each phase assist in the mitigation of vulnerabilities and management of risk.

Planning

In the first phase of the system development process, the need for a new system to achieve the business's strategic objectives is identified. This is a preliminary plan or a feasibility study for acquiring the resources to modify or improve a service. The purpose of this step is to determine the scope of the problem and identify solutions. The resources, costs, time and benefits should be considered at this stage.

The feasibility study should incorporate the following:

- Assessment of the impact on the existing environment.
- Staff development and resource requirements.
- Project development cost analysis.
- Programme maintenance costs.
- Evaluation of alternative project implementation approaches, such as build versus buy and outsourcing.
- Description of the proposed solution.
- Risks associated with the proposed solution.
- Benefit analysis, including cost reduction, error reduction, new customers and improved customer service.
- Involvement of information security teams to ensure that appropriate security concerns have been incorporated into the feasibility study.

Requirements

This phase defines how an organization will focus on the source of its problem or the need for a change. In the event of a problem, possible solutions should be submitted and analysed to identify the most appropriate ways to address the goals of the project.

Business and operational requirement specifications should be developed to ensure that the project requirements that are necessary to support business objectives are understood. Users and development teams generally lead this process. The business requirements should consider the following issues:

- Data that are required to support the system or application and how they relate to other data.
- Frequency of use of the system or application.
- Required response time for online processing.
- Function relations to and dependencies on other components.

- Identification of applicable legal or regulatory requirements or constraints.
- Anticipated life span of the system or application.

Operational requirements should consider the following issues:

- Security requirements.
- Contingency requirements.
- Distributed and centralized processing requirements.
- Data input strategy and responsibility.
- Data retention requirements.
- Output distribution requirements.
- Expected transaction volumes, including project transaction growth.
- Critical system performance requirements.

Information security teams should be involved throughout the business and operational requirements phase to ensure that security concerns are properly addressed and reflected in the requirements document. The risk-assessment methodology is performed mainly during this phase to provide early security perspectives for the project team.

Design

This phase involves describing the necessary specifications, features and operations that will satisfy the functional requirements of the proposed system. It includes the ability to transpose the business and operational requirements into functional requirements to reflect the anticipated user experience associated with the system or application. Functional specifications reflect the user's perspective, which has been translated into the preliminary design. For maintenance and enhancement activities, the focus is on using a before/after description to document what will change.

Functional specifications should include the following:

- Data flow diagrams: Tracing data through all their processing points.
- Data definitions: Defining data, data relationships and naming conventions.
- Screen definitions: Defining input fields and checking ranges.
- Inputs: Sources of inputs, types of data and description of data.
- Report definitions: Describing reports, the data to be contained in each report, how the data values are derived and the users who utilize specific reports.

- Control and security requirements: Inputting editing requirements, audit log trails for critical data from the point of origin to the point of disposition and audit log trails for the use of privileges and identifying critical processing areas.
- System interface requirements: Identifying interaction points between this system and other systems, anticipated inputs and outputs, response time expectations and other intersystem dependencies.
- Backup, restart and recovery: Determining the frequency of backup, rationale behind backup, backup retention requirements, restart requirements specifying how the application should be restarted and recovery requirements.
- Contingency requirements: Conducting an analysis to determine how long the application can be unavailable before the business is affected and identifying datasets, software and other items that need to be restored at an offsite processing centre.
- Hardware requirements: Determining communication requirements, disk space and processing equipment.
- Service-level requirements: Determining uptime requirements, required response times, critical windows, deadlines for input and deadlines for report distribution.
- Capacity requirements: Determining transaction volumes and expected growth.
- Conversion requirements: Developing a method to be used to create data on the new system, a method to reconcile data during conversion, cutover requirements and a process for verifying converted data.

During the functional specifications process, information security teams should generally be involved in supporting the project team's efforts to capture the preliminary design and functional description of the system or application. Functional specifications should include security-related information such as technical features—that is, access controls and operational practices (i.e., awareness and training). Information security teams should review and provide feedback on this document prior to the detailed design phase.

Development

This phase entails engaging the programmer, network engineer and/or database developer in the project. The work includes using a flow chart to ensure that the process is organized. The development phase signifies the end of the initial section of the process and the start of code development. Specifically, the code is produced according to the requirements produced in the design phase.

In the development phase, the system's or application's security features are developed, configured and enabled, and the programme specifications are used to describe the programme logic and processing requirements. The programme specifications are developed as part of this phase prior to the commencement of programming. These specifications provide the requirements necessary to determine the steps needed to code the programmes.

Information security teams should retain the right to perform source code reviews for critical aspects of the system or application, including user authentication, authorization and financial transactions. Source code reviews should have an enhanced focus on code provided by third parties, including offshore development organizations.

Testing

This phase involves system integration and system testing of programmes and procedures and is normally carried out by a quality assurance (QA) professional to determine whether the proposed design meets the initial set of business goals. Testing may be repeated, specifically to check for errors, bugs and interoperability, and should be performed until the end user finds the results acceptable. Another part of this phase is verification and validation, both of which will help ensure successful completion.

Unit testing

Unit testing is an integral part of the agile software development process that aims to identify and resolve bugs through a review of isolated sequences of code. The unit test criteria should include the following:

- File updating, merging and sorting.
- All decision logic.
- All system or application interfaces and integration testing.
- Invalid transactions and the related error-handling routines.
- Restart/recovery routines.
- Stress testing.
- Error conditions.
- Page counters and overflow headers.

System testing

During the system testing phase, code development for the project is completed, and testing is performed to ensure that all functions work as required.

The system test environment is typically shared among all programmers with strictly controlled changes to the environment. System test criteria should include the following:

- Verification that all functionality is performed as specified by the functional and design specifications.
- Programme interfaces.
- Other system interfaces.
- Restart and recovery procedures.
- Transaction validation and rejection.
- Transaction processing cycles.
- System or application performance criteria.
- System or application output generation.
- Stress testing.
- Error handling.
- Input/output verification.
- Procedures and restrictions regarding the use of production data.
- Complete and accurate audit log trails.
- Security testing—that is, authentication and authorization.
- System or application security testing—that is, ethical hacking.
- Code reviews of critical sections of code and externally developed code.

Where possible, system or application security testing should be executed using an automated testing tool. This will support the creation of tests and procedures that can be used for regression testing during future enhancements.

Parallel test plan

Where an existing system or application is in place, parallel testing ensures that the functions within a simulated production environment are equivalent to the existing process.

During the system testing phase, information security teams should be deeply involved in reviewing the security tests written by the project/test team and validating the security testing results. Security teams may also elect to perform a penetration test to ensure that the development team considers common security vulnerabilities.

Deployment

Deployment involves the actual installation of the newly developed system and/or application. This step puts the project into production by moving the data and components from the old system into the new system through a direct cutover. While this can be a complicated transition, the cutover typically occurs during off-peak hours, thus minimizing the risk.

The cutover/installation plan documents the transition from an old system or application to a new one. This plan should address any migration of production data that has not been performed. It should also address the installation activities and coordination with system users. Fallback procedures should be defined in the event of an erroneous transition.

Maintenance

This phase involves maintenance and requires regular updates. During this step, end users can refine the system to boost performance, add new capabilities or meet additional user requirements. It also includes a post-implementation review, conformance and defect tracking.

Post-implementation review

A post-implementation review ensures that the system or application is operating at a satisfactory level. This review involves soliciting user feedback on the overall effectiveness of the project and the achievement of the requirements and timelines. This information provides valuable insight for future projects and identifies potential shortcomings in the SDLC.

Security teams should participate in the post-implementation review to confirm that the security capabilities deployed are satisfactory.

At this time, the documentation of all security decisions made in support of the system or application is finalized, and variances from existing security policies and standards are noted. Where variances are permitted on a temporary basis, tracking is initiated to ensure that they are resolved in accordance with an agreed-upon schedule.

Conformance and defect tracking

The project management process should ensure conformance with all aspects of the SDLC. In this context, conformance refers to ensuring that the documents itemized earlier are created, reviewed and approved before the next phase of the SDLC.

Any modification to a document, once approved, should be reviewed, and all impacted groups should agree on the change. Defect-checking tools should be used to monitor and track identified defects during all testing phases. This provides a basis for making informed decisions regarding the status and resolution of any defects.

Secure software development lifecycle

The secure software development lifecycle (SSDLC) is the process of including security artefacts in the SDLC process.

An SSDLC is a framework that defines the process used by organizations to build an application from its inception to decommission. Throughout the years, multiple standard SDLC models have been proposed (waterfall, iterative, agile) and integrated into various organizational environments via multiple ways.

Planning and requirements

The first step in any initiative is to map out a planning process. During this phase, an organization must identify the release theme, contents and timeline. This phase typically includes activities such as collecting end-user

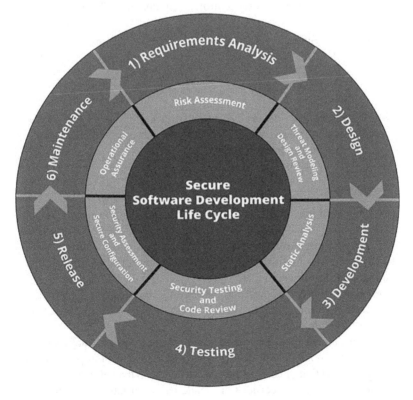

Figure 5.2 The elements within the secure software development lifecycle (Digital Maelstrom, 2020).

requirements, determining user stories to include in the release, and planning release phases and dates.

Key considerations during this phase include the following:

- Ensuring that an application meets business requirements.
- Engaging in threat modelling/secure design.
- Choosing the language and libraries to use in the development process.
- Mapping test cases to business and functional requirements.

Architecture and design

In the architecture and design phase, the organization's technology teams should follow the architecture and design guidelines to address identified risks. In addition, this phase evaluates the planned system design and potential integration with other systems, as well as the incorporation of shared services and common security controls, including the following:

- Authentication.
- Disaster recovery (DR).
- Intrusion detection.
- Incident reporting.

When vulnerabilities are addressed early in the design phase, processes include threat modelling and architecture risk analysis to assist in simplifying and providing a secure development process.

Test planning

Applying security controls in the testing phase should be considered carefully and planned logically. The intent is to integrate the controls into existing systems; therefore, challenges to system performance should be discovered early. Additionally, some security controls may limit or hinder normal development activities.

For new information systems, the security requirements identified and described in the appropriate system security plans should be designed, developed and implemented.

System security plans for operational information systems may require the development of additional security controls to supplement in-place controls or the modification of controls that are deemed less than effective.

During this phase, decisions are made based on integration challenges and trade-offs. It is important to document major decisions and business/technology drivers.

In cases where the application of a planned control is not possible or advisable, compensatory controls should be considered and documented.

Coding

During the development phase, the organization's development teams should train developers in secure coding practices. While performing the usual code review to ensure that the project has the specified features and functions, developers should minimize security vulnerabilities introduced in the code by integrating secure coding practices—that is, OWASP. Specifically, the source code should be periodically reviewed using automated tools or manual spot checks for common programming errors that have a detrimental impact on system security, including the following:

- Cross-site scripting vulnerabilities.
- Buffer overflows.
- Race conditions.
- Object model violations.
- Poor user input validation and error handling.
- Exposed security parameters.
- Passwords in the clear.
- Violations of stated security policy, models or architecture as part of the software development QA process.
- Using open-source components in a secure way.
- Static code analysis.
- Vulnerability scanning.

Testing and results

To reduce redundant functional and security testing activities, the following recommendations are made:

- Functional test plans should include general security feature testing to the greatest extent possible.
- Preliminary testing of basic security controls should be performed during functional testing to reduce or eliminate issues earlier in the development cycle—that is, mandatory access controls, secure code development and firewalls.
- Preliminary testing is considered development-level testing, not certification and accreditation (C&A) testing, and if no changes occur, test results should be reused to the greatest extent possible in the C&A.

56 *System development lifecycle*

- For systems of high visibility and sensitivity, independent development testing should be considered.
- Preliminary testing should be completed at the component or security zone level to ensure that each component or security zone is secure as an entity.
- The process and results of all security testing that occurs throughout the lifecycle should be captured for evaluation, issue identification and potential reuse.

The following vulnerability assessments should also be considered during this phase:

- Dynamic code analysis.
- Penetration testing.
- Ethical hacking.
- Password hacking.

Release and maintenance

After deployment and implementation, security practices should be followed throughout software maintenance. Applications should be regularly updated and assessed as follows:

- Security assessment.
- Vulnerability scanning.
- Penetration testing.
- Ethical hacking.

Cloud environments

Vulnerability management is the process of identifying, classifying, remediating and mitigating vulnerabilities, especially in software and firmware. This process becomes complex in a cloud-based environment, as various layers of technology can be managed by different organizations based on the implementation. An organization's vulnerability management programme should extend to ensuring that vendor-managed cloud-based solutions have appropriate controls in place to align with the organization's risk appetite and risk tolerance.

Vulnerability scanning in a cloud environment

The differences between traditional technology environments and cloud-based environments arise primarily from (1) an organization outsourcing the ability to own and control the infrastructure for cloud services to an external vendor and (2) the organization being unable to access the vulnerability data of native cloud services. There is an inability to associate the data with cloud-native vulnerabilities, as CVE IDs are not generally assigned to them. Therefore, it becomes difficult for organizations as clients to make informed, risk-based decisions regarding vulnerable cloud services. For example, when should the organization decide to reject the risk and stop using a cloud service or accept the risk and continue using the service?

Furthermore, even if CVE IDs are assigned to cloud-native vulnerabilities, the differences between traditional and cloud environments are so vast that vulnerability data that are normally associated with a CVE in a traditional environment are inadequate for cloud service vulnerabilities. For example, in a traditional IT environment, CVEs are linked to a software version, and the organization can determine whether a software application is vulnerable by checking the version. In cloud services, the software version is usually known only to the cloud service provider. Therefore, the organization as a client may be unable to apply security controls or other mitigations to address the risk of a vulnerability.

Owing to these differences, the cloud provider should consider including vulnerability data that are useful in the context of a cloud service. Specifically, vulnerability data provided by the cloud provider would provide the organization with the ability to make risk-based decisions, including whether to continue or stop using a cloud service.

> EXAMPLE: Vulnerability Scanning in Amazon Web Services Elastic Container Registry.

The Amazon Web Services (AWS) Electric Container Registry (ECR) is a fully managed container registry that makes it easy for developers to store, manage and deploy container images. Image scanning is an automated vulnerability assessment feature in an ECR that helps improve the security of an organization's application container images by scanning them for a broad range of OS vulnerabilities.

Implement image scanning for containers

Container security comprises a range of activities and tools involving developers, security operations engineers and infrastructure administrators. One crucial link in the cloud-native supply chain is scanning container images for vulnerabilities and obtaining actionable insights. ECR image scanning uses the ECR native solution and provides an implementation strategy for a specific use case and scheduled re-scans as the foundation.

Prevent images with known vulnerabilities from entering production

An organization can enable image scans or push for its repositories to ensure that every image is automatically checked against an aggregated set of CVEs. The AWS ECR uses the severity of a CVE from an upstream distribution source if available; otherwise, the common vulnerability scoring system (CVSS) score can be used to obtain the National Vulnerability Database vulnerability severity rating. This can assist an organization with automated detection and responses to container image vulnerabilities prior to promoting and deploying an image into production.

There are two kinds of scanning:

Static scanning is performed in environments prior to deployment with the implication that developers (or secops) can detect vulnerabilities before a container is launched. ECR image scanning falls under this category; that is, it enables an organization to scan OS packages in container images for CVEs, a public list of known security threats, without the need for an organization to set up its own scanning infrastructure or purchase third-party scanning licences.

Dynamic scanning is executed in a runtime environment and identifies vulnerabilities for containers running in test, QA or production environments, making it possible to identify vulnerabilities introduced by software installed post-build as well as zero-day vulnerabilities. For dynamic (or runtime) container security, there is an array of options

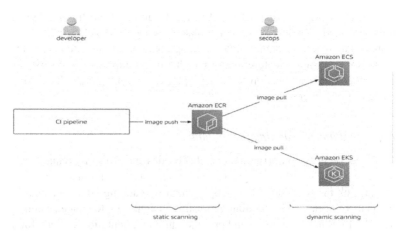

Figure 5.3 Native container image scanning in Amazon ECR (AWS, 2019).

provided by third parties, from open-source solutions such as CNCF Falco to offerings through AWS container competency partners, including Aqua Security, Trend Micro and Twistlock.

Once applications are in production, verify that they remain vulnerability free. An organization can also scan images using an application programmable interface (API) command, allowing it to set up periodic scans for running container images to ensure continued monitoring. ECR sends a notification when a scan is completed, and the results are available in the console and over the API.

Use case

This use case shows scheduled re-scans of container images used in a production environment. For example, the individual is in a secop role, looking after several ECR repositories, and rather than manually scanning images and reviewing the detailed findings of the image scans, he or she may use a high-level overview and the ability to drill down on a per-repository basis. The sample setup consists of four lambda functions, providing an HTTP API for managing scan configurations and taking care of scheduling the image scans, as well as an S3 bucket for storing the scan configurations:

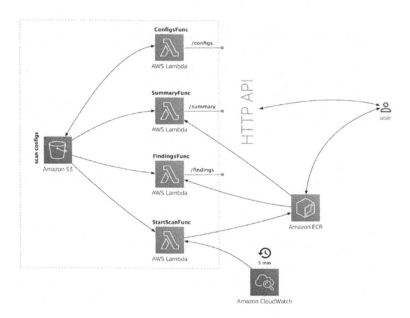

Figure 5.4 Native container image scanning in Amazon ECR (AWS, 2019).

Auditing configuration management

Securely configuring an organization's cloud technology environment is a responsibility shared between the organization and AWS. The organization provides requirements for secure configuration settings and expects AWS to provide a mechanism to implement and regularly audit the configurations in place.

Risk-management practice – DevOps

DevOps is a term used to describe better communication and collaboration between application development professionals and infrastructure operations professionals. It refers to a set of emerging practices to enable developers and operations professionals to work together. Developers want to release software more frequently, while operations professionals want to protect the stability of the infrastructure. DevOps is a business strategy of overlapping traditional operational and developmental lanes to create an environment that continually improves operations through the cross-pollination of developers and operators. The overall strategic objective of DevOps is to maximize investment outcomes and ensure that customers continually receive increased service quality and features in a manner that satisfies their needs. This analysis will focus on integrating risk-management practices into the DevOps framework.

The overall goal of DevOps is to improve the business value of the work completed in IT and to focus on the following goals:

- Deliver measurable business value through continuous and high-quality service delivery.
- Emphasize simplicity and agility in all areas, including technology, process and human factors.
- Break down barriers between development and operations by enabling trust and sharing. ownership, supporting innovation and encouraging collaboration.
- Manage dynamic compliance, as access/sharing laws change rapidly.

DevOps represents a change in IT culture, focusing on rapid IT service delivery through the adoption of agile, lean practices in the context of a system-oriented approach. DevOps emphasizes people (and culture) and seeks to improve collaboration between operations and development teams. DevOps implementations utilize technology—especially automation tools that can leverage an increasingly programmable and dynamic infrastructure from a lifecycle perspective.

Gartner

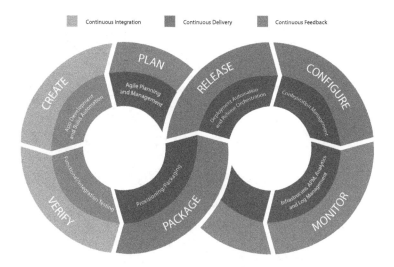

Figure 5.5 Elements within the DevOps process (AWS, 2019).

1 Agile and lean refer to teams iterating, with short development cycles and fast feedback. Agile focuses on culture and is agnostic in regard to the tools used.

2 DevOps refers to how engineering organizations collaborate using cross-functional teams. DevOps starts with culture and drives towards tooling.

3 System reliability engineering (SRE) refers to how engineering organizations automate, entrusting highly scaled operations to people with a software engineering mindset. SRE starts with tooling and drives towards culture.

4 DevOps variants (such as "SecDevOps") involve the insertion or addition of another organization/practice early in the SDLC, and the prevalence of these different types of DevOps speaks to the increasing integration of functions in modern organizations.

DevOps incorporates many variations on the theme. However, most observers would agree that the following capabilities are common to virtually all DevOps cultures: (1) collaboration, (2) automation, (3) continuous integration, (4) continuous delivery, (5) continuous testing, (6) continuous monitoring and (7) rapid remediation.

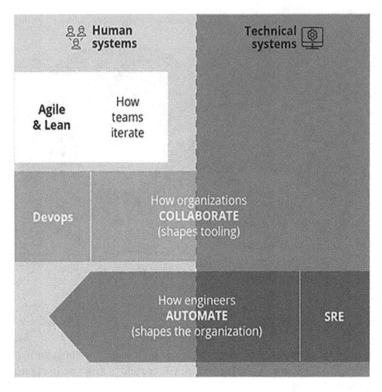

Figure 5.6 The elements of SecDevOps (Humble & Molesky, 2011).

Collaboration

Development and IT operations work together, and DevOps extends far beyond the IT organization due to the need for collaboration, which extends to all stakeholders in the delivery of software.

"The foundation of DevOps success is how well teams and individuals collaborate across the enterprise to get things done more rapidly, efficiently and effectively" – Tony Bradley, "Scaling Collaboration in DevOps", DevOps.com.

Automation

DevOps relies heavily on automation and tools and on toolchains to automate large parts of the end-to-end software development and deployment process.

Health - Status Security Tools / Services	Web - Application Development Tools / Services	Operating System (OS) Tools / Services	Governance Validation Management Tools / Services	Infrastructure Platform Tools / Services
Monitoring Alerting Trending	Application Servers	Linus Compilers & Debuggers	Application Development	IAAS & PAAS
Security	Databases	Unix Compilers & Debuggers	Configuration Management	Webservers
Process	Visualization Platform	Windows Compilers & Debuggers	Test & Build	Queues & Caches
Logging		MAC OS		Containerization Tools

Figure 5.7 Tools and services for DevOps (Humble & Molesky, 2011).

Continuous integration

Continuous integration is essential in DevOps cultures because DevOps emerged from an agile culture, and continuous integration is a fundamental tenet of the agile approach:

> A cornerstone of DevOps is continuous integration (CI), a technique designed and named by Grady Booch that continually merges source code updates from all developers on a team into a shared mainline. This continual merging prevents a developer's local copy of a software project from drifting too far afield as new code is added by others, avoiding catastrophic merge conflicts.
> – Aaron Cois, "Continuous Integration in DevOps", DevOps blog, Software Engineering Institute, Carnegie Mellon

The continuous integration principle of agile development has cultural implications for the development group. Forcing developers to integrate their work into other developers' work frequently, at least daily, exposes integration issues and conflicts much earlier than the waterfall development approach. However, to achieve this benefit, developers must communicate with each other much more frequently.

Continuous testing

The testing piece of DevOps is easy to overlook, according to Gartner: "Given the rising cost and impact of software failures, you can't afford to unleash a release that could disrupt the existing user experience or introduce new features that expose the organization to new security, reliability, or compliance risks".

Continuous testing is not just a QA function; in fact, it starts in the development environment. Developers build quality into the code and provide test data sets. QA engineers configure automation test cases and the testing environment.

On the QA side, speed is essential. Test engineers meet the challenge of quick turnaround not only by automating the test process but also by redefining test methodologies:

> Continuous testing creates a central system of decisions that helps you assess the business risk each application presents to your organization. Applied consistently, it guides development teams to meet business expectations and provides managers visibility to make informed trade-off decisions to optimize the business value of a release candidate.
>
> –Continuous Testing for IT Leaders, Parasoft.

Operations can ensure that monitoring tools are in place and test environments are properly configured. They can participate in functional, load, stress and leak tests and offer analysis based on their experience with similar applications running in production.

The test function in a DevOps environment helps developers balance quality and speed. Using automated tools reduces the cost of testing and allows test engineers to leverage their time more effectively. Most importantly, continuous testing shortens test cycles by allowing integration testing earlier in the process.

Continuous testing also eliminates testing bottlenecks through virtualized, dependent services and simplifies the creation of virtualized test environments that can be easily deployed, shared and updated as systems change. These capabilities reduce the cost of provisioning and maintaining test environments and shorten test cycle times by allowing integration testing earlier in the lifecycle.

Continuous delivery

The team at AWS defines continuous delivery as a DevOps "software development practice where code changes are automatically built, tested and prepared for a release to production". It expands upon continuous integration by deploying all code changes to a testing environment and/or a production environment after the build stage. When continuous delivery is implemented properly, developers will always have a deployment-ready built artefact that has passed through a standardized test process.

The actual release frequency can vary greatly depending on the company's legacy and goals. High-performing organizations using DevOps achieve multiple deployments per day compared to medium-performing organizations who release once per week to once per month.

Exactly what is released varies depending on the organization. In some organizations, QA and operations triage potential releases: (1) many go directly to users, (2) some go back to development, and (3) a few simply are not deployed at all. In comparison, other organizations push everything that comes from developers out to users, counting on real-time monitoring and rapid remediation to minimize the impact of a rare failure. It is important to note that because each update is small, the chance of any one of them causing a failure is significantly reduced.

Continuous delivery enables businesses to reduce the cycle time to obtain faster feedback from users, reduce the risk and cost of deployments, gain visibility of the delivery process itself and manage the risks of software delivery more effectively.

From a risk and compliance perspective, continuous delivery is a more mature, efficient and effective method of applying controls to meet regulatory requirements than the traditional combination of automated and manual activities.

Continuous monitoring

Given the sheer number of releases in a continuous delivery environment, it is difficult to implement the rigorous pre-release testing typically required in waterfall development approaches. In a DevOps environment, failures must be found and fixed in real time. With continuous monitoring, teams measure the performance and availability of software to improve stability. Continuous monitoring helps identify the root causes of issues quickly to proactively prevent outages and minimize user issues. Some monitoring experts even advocate that the definition of a service must include monitoring, as it is viewed as integral to service delivery.

Similar to testing, monitoring starts in development. The same tools used to monitor the production environment can be employed in development to identify performance problems before a product moves into production. Two kinds of monitoring are required for DevOps: (1) server monitoring and (2) application performance monitoring.

Integration of risk-management practices in DevOps

Through 2015, 80% of the risks associated with attaining DevOps programme objectives stemmed from how organizational change was managed.

The risk-management process shows how to evaluate, starting with the absence of internal controls, which is known as inherent risk. With the inclusion of proper code certification, which indicates that the overall system works as intended and that its environment protects it from undue influences, the risk is mitigated. Secure capabilities allow stakeholders to take proactive actions such as quarantining, meaning moving or deleting sensitive or non-public information from their network before it negatively impacts their capabilities through unauthorized exposure and results in a brand, reputational, financial, legal or cybersecurity risk to the business. Stakeholders should be empowered to do the following:

- Continuously monitor all networks and automate actions.
- Discover, classify and act on all transactions involving data that have been identified as sensitive, critical or confidential to create information privacy solutions.
- Facilitate compliance with all laws and regulations that apply to data, users and transactions based on local and global laws as they apply.
- Scale with information and footprint growth and provide data protection in a timely and cost-effective manner that allows for predictable constant mission outcomes.
- Easily install, deploy and update in a reasonable time frame to all appliances that are utilized by the organization in a manner that does not interrupt end-user expectations.
- Minimize the need for IT oversight by creating automated pre-defined actions for information privacy solutions and data loss prevention.
- Optimally, develop a data security and data privacy dashboard similar to and integrated with network management systems.
- Provide daily, weekly, monthly and annual reports that can be used to satisfy audit requests.
- Reduce business risk and liability.

A common reason for not implementing DevOps and continuous delivery in IT organizations is that this approach does not comply with industry standards and regulations unless the risk-management process is considered. Two controls that are often cited are the segregation of duties and change management.

Regulations and standards require organizations to prove that they know what is happening and why. Therefore, protecting information and services and performing accurate reporting are essential. Compliance with authorities to acquire certain data and the mechanisms employed to secure the data acquired are at the forefront of many discussions today. Most IT organizations are subject to regulation and implement controls to ensure that they comply. Controls are also essential in reducing the risk of loss, which may affect the confidentiality, integrity, availability and privacy of information.

Leveraging a risk-management approach would facilitate an understanding of the residual risk once internal controls are implemented. This would allow the business to gain an understanding of the alignment of residual risk with its risk profile.

6 Risk-management practice – business continuity management

A business continuity management (BCM) programme manages an organization's risk of business disruption through the implementation of IT readiness for business continuity. A failure of ICT services may potentially result in security issues, such as system intrusion and malware infections. The organization's ICT readiness for business continuity (IRBC) is based on ISO 27031 and includes incident preparedness, DR planning and emergency response and management.

BCM is a holistic management process that identifies potential threats to the continuity of an organization's business activities and provides a framework for building resilience and capability through an effective response that safeguards the interests of the organization from disruptions.

As part of an organization's BCM process, IRBC is a component of the programme.

IRBC focuses on the management of one or more systems that complement and support the organization's BCM programme to improve the organization's readiness for the following:

- Respond to the constantly changing risk environment.
- Ensure the continuation of critical business operations supported by the related ICT services.
- Be ready to respond before an ICT service disruption occurs upon detection of one or a series of related events that become incidents.
- Respond to and recover from incidents/disasters and failures.

Figure 6.1 The business continuity process (phoenixNAP, 2020).

DOI: 10.4324/9781003200895-6

Key principles

An organization's BCM programme should be based on the following key principles:

- Incident prevention – Protecting ITS from threats, such as environmental and hardware failures, operational errors, malicious attacks and natural disasters, is critical to maintaining an organization's desired level of system availability.
- Incident detection – Incidents should be detected at the earliest opportunity to minimize the impact on services, reduce recovery efforts and preserve the quality of service.
- Response – Responding to an incident in the most appropriate manner will lead to a more efficient recovery and minimize downtime.
- Recovery – Identifying and implementing the appropriate recovery strategy ensures the timely resumption of services and maintains the integrity of data. Understanding the recovery priorities allows the most critical services to be reinstated first. Services of a less critical nature may be reinstated later or, in some circumstances, decommissioned.
- Improvement – Lessons learned from small and large incidents should be documented, analysed and reviewed. Understanding these lessons will allow an organization to better prepare for, control and avoid incidents and disruption.

Key elements

The key elements of the organization's IRBC can be summarized as follows:

People: Specialists with appropriate skills and knowledge and competent backup personnel.
Facilities: The physical environment in which ICT resources are located.
Technology:

- Hardware, including racks, servers, storage arrays, tape devices and fixtures.
- Network, including data connectivity, voice services, switches and routers.
- Software, including OS, application software, links or interfaces between them.
- Applications and batch processing routines.
- Data: application data, voice data and other types of data.

- Processes such as supporting documentation to describe the configuration of ICT resources and enable the effective operation, recovery and maintenance of those services.

Suppliers: Other components of end-to-end services where ICT service provision is dependent upon an external service provider or another organization within the supply chain—that is, a financial market data provider, telecom carrier or Internet service provider.

Establishing an organization's ICT readiness using the plan perform check act

Policy

An organization's IRBC policy provides documented principles to which it will aspire and against which its effectiveness can be measured. It should

- establish and demonstrate the commitment of management to an IRBC programme,
- include or refer to the organization's IRBC objectives,

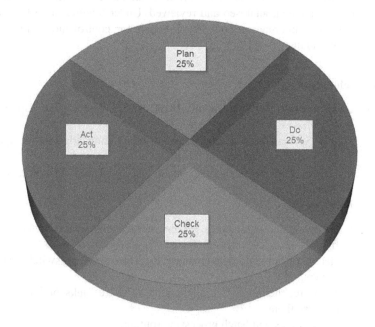

Figure 6.2 The elements of the ICT readiness process (ISO, 2020).

- define the scope of IRBC, including limitations and exclusions,
- be approved and signed off on by management,
- be communicated to appropriate internal and external stakeholders,
- identify and provide relevant authorities for the availability of resources such as the budget and personnel necessary to perform activities in line with the IRBC policy and
- be reviewed at planned intervals and when significant changes, such as environmental changes or changes in the organization's business and structure, occur.

Planning

The main objective of the planning phase is to establish the organization's ICT readiness requirements, including the following:

- The IRBC strategy and IRBC plan that are required to support the legal, statutory and regulatory requirements relating to the defined scope and the achievement of the organization's business continuity aims and objectives.
- The performance criteria needed by the organization to monitor the degree of ICT readiness required to achieve those aims and objectives.

Resources

As part of the policy mandate, the organization defines the need for an IRBC programme as part of its overall BCM objectives and determines and provides the resources needed to establish, implement, operate and maintain the IRBC programme.

IRBC roles, responsibilities, competencies and authorities should be defined and documented.

Management should perform the following tasks:

- Appoint or nominate a person with appropriate seniority and authority to be accountable for IRBC policy and implementation.
- Appoint one or more competent persons who, irrespective of other responsibilities, should implement the elements of this programme.
- Maintain the IRBC management system as described by the programme.

Competency of staff

The organization should ensure that all personnel who are assigned IRBC responsibilities are competent to perform the required tasks.

Defining requirements

As part of its BCM programme, the organization should categorize its activities according to their priority for continuity, as determined by a business impact analysis, and define the minimum level at which each critical activity needs to be performed.

Management should agree upon the organization's business continuity requirements, and these requirements will result in recovery time objectives (RTOs) and recovery point objectives (RPOs) for the minimum business continuity objective (MBCO) per product, service or activity. RTOs start from the point at which a disruption occurs and run until the product, service or activity resumes.

Understanding critical services

There may be several ICT services that are critical and required to enable recovery to take place. Each of these critical ICT services should have its own documented RTO and RPO for the MBCO of the ICT service. The objectives may include aspects of ICT service delivery, such as the help-desk. The RTO of critical ICT services will invariably be a lower priority than the RTO of business continuity. The organization should identify and document its critical ICT services to include brief descriptions and names that are meaningful to the organization at the service user level. This will ensure a common understanding between business and ICT staff, as different names may be used for the same ICT service. Each critical ICT service listed should identify the product or service that it supports, and management should agree upon the ICT services and the associated IRBC requirements.

For each critical ICT service identified and agreed upon, all ICT components of the end-to-end service should be described and documented to show how they are configured or linked to deliver each service. Both the normal ICT service delivery environment and the ICT continuity service delivery environment configurations should be documented.

For each critical ICT service, the current continuity capability—that is, the existence of a single point of failure—should be reviewed from a prevention perspective to assess the risks of service interruption or degradation, which can be taken as part of the overall BCM risk-assessment exercise. Opportunities to improve ICT service resilience and thereby lower the likelihood and/or impact of service disruption should also be sought. This type of review may also highlight opportunities to enable early detection and reaction to ICT service disruption. The organization can decide whether there is a business case for investing in identified opportunities to improve service resilience. This risk assessment, which may form part of the organization's overall risk-management framework, may also inform the business case for enhancing ICT service recovery capability.

Identifying gaps between ICT readiness capabilities and business continuity requirements

For each critical ICT service, the current ICT readiness arrangements, such as prevention, monitoring, detection, response and recovery, should be compared with business continuity requirements, and any gaps should be documented.

Management should be informed of any gaps between critical IRBC capability and business continuity requirements. Such gaps might indicate risks and the need for additional resilience and recovery resources, such as the following:

- Staff, including numbers, skills and knowledge.
- Facilities to house ICT equipment—that is, a computer room.
- Supporting technology, plant, equipment and networks.
- Information applications and databases.
- Finance or budget allocation.
- External services and suppliers.

Management should sign-off on the ICT service definitions, the documented list of critical ICT services and the risks associated with identified gaps between critical IRBC capability and business continuity requirements.

This should include, where appropriate, signing off on identified risks. The options for addressing the identified gaps and risks should then be explored by determining IRBC strategies.

Determining IRBC strategy options

IRBC strategies should define the approaches to implement the required resilience strategies so that the principles of incident prevention, detection, response, recovery and restoration are in place.

A full range of IRBC strategy options should be evaluated. The strategies chosen should support the business continuity requirements of the organization.

The organization should consider implementation and ongoing resource requirements when developing the strategy. External suppliers may be contracted to provide specialized services and skills that play an important role in supporting the strategy.

The IRBC strategy should be flexible enough to cater to different business strategies in different markets.

In addition, the strategy should consider internal constraints and factors, such as the following:

- Budget.
- Resource availability.
- Potential costs and benefits.
- Technological constraints.
- The organization's risk appetite.
- The organization's existing IRBC strategy.
- Regulatory obligations.

IRBC strategy options

The organization should consider a range of options for the incident readiness of its critical ICT services. The options should allow for increasing protection and resilience as well as providing for recovery and restoration from an unplanned disruption and may include an internal arrangement. Services delivered to the organization may be provided externally by one or more third parties.

The options should consider the various components required to ensure the continuity and recovery of critical ICT services.

Skills and knowledge

The organization should identify appropriate strategies for maintaining core ICT skills and knowledge. This may extend beyond employees to contractors and other stakeholders who possess extensive ICT specialist skills and knowledge. Strategies to protect or provide those skills may include the following:

- Documentation of the way in which critical ICT services are performed.
- Multiskill training of ICT staff and contractors to enhance skill redundancy.
- Separation of core skills to reduce the concentration of risk.
- Knowledge retention and management.

Facilities

According to the identified risks, the organization should devise strategies to reduce the impact of the unavailability of normal ICT facilities.

These may include one or more of the following:

- Alternative facilities within the organization, including displacement of other activities.
- Alternative facilities provided by other organizations.
- Alternative facilities provided by third-party specialists.
- Working from home or at other remote sites.
- Other agreed-upon suitable working facilities.
- Use of an alternative workforce at an established site.
- Alternative facilities that can be transported to the site of the disruption and used to directly replace some of the physical assets involved.

Strategies for ICT facilities can vary significantly, and a range of options may be available. Different types of incidents or threats may require the implementation of multiple strategies that will be driven in part by the organization's size, breadth of activities, locations, technologies and budget.

In considering the use of alternative premises, the following should be considered:

- Site security.
- Staff access.
- Proximity to existing facilities.
- Availability.

Technology

The ICT services upon which critical business activities depend should be available in advance of the resumption of the dependent critical business activities. The required solutions should ensure the availability of applications within specific time frames; that is, the RTOs should be determined as part of the business impact analysis (BIA). Technology platforms and application software should be put in place within time frames demanded by the organization. Technologies that support critical ICT services frequently require complex arrangements to ensure continuity, and the following should be considered when selecting IRBC strategies:

- RTOs and RPOs for critical ICT services that support the critical activities identified by the BCM programme.
- Location and distance between technology sites.
- Number of technology sites.
- Remote access to systems.
- Cooling requirements.

- Power requirements.
- Use of unstaffed sites.
- Telecoms connectivity and redundant routing.
- The nature of "fallback"—that is, manual or automatic intervention—that is required to activate alternative ICT provision.
- Level of automation required.
- Technology obsolescence.
- Outsourced service provider connectivity and other external links.

Data

Additionally, critical business activities may depend on the provision of up-to-date or near-up-to-date data. Data continuity solutions should be designed to meet the RPOs of each critical business activity of the organization as they relate to critical business activities. The selected IRBC options should ensure the ongoing confidentiality, integrity and availability of critical data that support critical activities. Data storage and IRBC strategies should meet the organization's business continuity requirements and should consider the following:

- How data are securely stored—that is, disk, tape or optical media; appropriate backup and restoration mechanisms should be in place to ensure that the data are secure and in a safe environment.
- Where information is stored, transported or transmitted, distance; location, network links, onsite, offsite or third party; and expected time frames for the retrieval of backup media.
- Restoration time frame, driven by the volume of data, how they are stored and the complexity of the technical restoration process along with the requirements of service users and the needs of organizational continuity.

An understanding of the "end-to-end" use of data throughout the organization is critical and may include information feeds to and from third parties.

Processes

In selecting its IRBC strategy, the organization should consider the processes necessary to ensure the viability of that strategy, including those necessary in incident prevention, incident detection, incident response and DR. The organization should also identify any factors necessary for the effective implementation of those individual processes—that is, key skill sets, critical data, key enabling technologies or critical equipment/facilities.

Suppliers

The organization should identify and document external dependencies that support ICT service provision and take adequate steps to ensure that critical equipment and services can be provided by its suppliers within predetermined and agreed-upon time frames. Such dependencies may exist for hardware, software, telecoms, applications, third-party hosting services, utilities and environmental issues, such as air conditioning, environmental monitoring and fire suppression.

Strategies for these services may include the following:

- Storage of additional equipment and software copies at another location.
- Arrangements with suppliers for the delivery of replacement equipment at short notice.
- Rapid repair and/or replacement of faulty parts in the event of an equipment malfunction.
- Dual supply of utilities such as power and telecoms.
- Emergency generating equipment.
- Identification of alternative/substitute suppliers.

The organization should include ICT and BCM requirements in contracts with its partners and service providers. Contract schedules should include reference to each party's obligations, agreed-upon service levels, response to major incidents, cost assignment, exercising frequency and corrective actions.

Signing off

The selected IRBC strategy options should be presented to management with recommendations for a decision based on risk appetite and cost. Managers should be advised whether the selected IRBC strategy options are unable to meet the business continuity requirements, in which case they should be informed of current capability. Managers should select the IRBC strategies from the options presented to them and approve and sign-off on the documented options to confirm that the options have been properly undertaken and support the overall business continuity requirements.

The selected IRBC strategy options should

- cater to the likely risks and effects of disruption,
- be integrated with the organization's chosen business continuity strategies and
- be appropriate for meeting the organization's overall objectives within its risk appetite.

Enhancing IRBC capability

Enhancing resilience

The organization should include within its high-level IRBC strategy and plans reference to specific enhancements of its IRBC capabilities, which are required to fulfil its identified IRBC requirements. These enhancements may be achieved through preventative and corrective actions as well as other specific processes or methodologies that are relevant responses to the organization's BIA and risk appetite.

ICT readiness performance criteria

Identification of performance criteria

Within any ICT environment, there are many potentially threatening events, such as hardware failures and security intrusion, and the organization should be capable of monitoring the threats and understanding whether the IRBC system is capable of adequately addressing them. The organization should therefore define performance criteria to measure the effectiveness of its ICT readiness. These criteria can be used to determine the desired quality of the response to a disruption in terms of both its effectiveness and efficiency. Performance criteria for IRBC should be based on the IRBC requirements as well as overall BCM objectives in terms of incident response and continuity requirements.

Implementing the elements of IRBC strategies

Awareness, skills and knowledge

General awareness of the readiness of the elements of ICT services to include people, facilities, technology, data, processes and suppliers, as well as their critical components, is crucial in ensuring the required support for the business continuity governance and management system, including ICT readiness.

The organization should therefore:

- Raise, enhance and maintain awareness through an ongoing education and information programme for relevant staff and establish a process for evaluating the effectiveness of awareness delivery.
- Ensure that staff are aware of how they contribute to the achievement of IRBC objectives.

The organization should ensure that all personnel who are assigned IRBC management responsibilities are competent to perform the required tasks by

- determining the necessary competencies for such personnel,
- conducting training needs analysis of such personnel,
- providing training,
- ensuring that the necessary competence has been achieved and
- maintaining records of education, training, skills, experience and qualifications.

Facilities

ICT recovery systems and critical data should, where possible, be physically separated from the operational site to prevent them from being affected by the same incident. The location of all ICT environments should be considered when implementing the strategy. For example, if possible, training or development ICT systems should be logically separated from production systems, as there may be an opportunity for these systems to be reconfigured in the event of a disaster to quickly restore production services.

The overall scalability, manageability, supportability, performance and cost characteristics of the different implementation techniques should be examined to identify those that are most appropriate for the chosen strategies and support the overall business continuity aims and objectives.

Technology

ICT technology strategies should be implemented and may include one or more of the following implementations and arrangements:

- Hot standby, where ICT infrastructure is replicated across two sites.
- Warm standby, where recovery takes place at a secondary site where ICT infrastructure is partially prepared.
- Cold standby, where infrastructure is built or configured from scratch at an alternative location.
- Ship-in arrangements, with external service providers providing hardware.
- Composite arrangement of the preceding strategies: a "pick-and-mix" approach.

Information security

The organization's information security requirements should be included in planning for business continuity and DR. An organization should ensure that documented plans and response and recovery procedures are developed and approved, detailing how the organization will manage a disruptive event and maintain its information security to a predetermined level based on management-approved information security continuity objectives.

According to an organization's information security continuity requirements, the organization should establish, document, implement and maintain the following:

- Information security controls within business continuity or DR processes, procedures and supporting systems and tools.
- Processes, procedures and implementation changes to maintain existing information security.
- Controls during an adverse situation.
- Compensatory controls for information security controls that cannot be maintained during an adverse situation.

Information processing facilities should be implemented with redundancy sufficient to meet availability requirements. The organization should identify business requirements for the availability of information systems. Where availability cannot be guaranteed using the existing systems architecture, redundant components or architectures should be considered.

Where applicable, redundant information systems should be tested to ensure that failover from one component to another component works as intended.

Data

The arrangements for the availability of data should be aligned with the requirements identified within the IRBC management strategies and may include the following:

- Additional data storage in a format that ensures data availability within the time frame identified in the business continuity programme.
- Alternative locations for data storage that may be physical or virtual, provided that the security and confidentiality of the data are maintained.
- Appropriate access procedures: if arrangements are made through third parties for the storage of information, the information owners should satisfy themselves that the appropriate controls are in place.

Processes

IRBC processes should be documented clearly, and in enough detail, to enable competent staff to execute them. Some of these processes may differ from daily operations. IRBC procedures may be dependent on the situation that unfolds and, in practice, may need to be adapted based on the disruption—that is, the degree of loss or damage, the organization's operational priorities and stakeholders' demands.

Suppliers

The organization should ensure that critical suppliers are able to support the IRBC service capabilities required by the organization. These suppliers should have their own documented and tested business continuity and IRBC plans with the capacity to support concurrent activations of incident or recovery plans by customers. The organization should establish a process to evaluate the capacity and capability of suppliers before engaging in their services and should continuously monitor and review the ability of suppliers after engaging them. Compliance with requirements/good practices in relevant standards is a useful means of determining suppliers' capability—for example, the adoption of ISO/IEC 24762 best practices by suppliers hosting/managing an alternate processing facility and providing ICT DR services.

Incident response

For any ICT incident, there should be an incident response to

* confirm the nature and extent of the incident,
* take control of the situation,
* contain the incident and
* communicate with stakeholders.

The incident response should trigger an appropriate IRBC action. This response should be integrated with the overall BCM incident response and may invoke an incident management team. Individuals responsible for incident management should have plans for the activation, operation, coordination and communication of the incident response.

IRBC plan documents

The organization should have documentation to manage potential disruption and thereby enable the continuity of ICT services and the recovery of critical activities. ICT incident management, business continuity and technical recovery plans may be activated in rapid succession or simultaneously. The organization may develop specific plan documents to recover or resume ICT services and return to a "normal" state. However, it might not be possible to define what "normal" looks like until sometime after the incident; therefore, it might not be possible to implement recovery plans immediately. The organization should therefore ensure that continuity arrangements are capable of extended operation in support of wider business continuity, allowing time for the development of "back-to-normal" recovery plans.

Content of plan documents

The organization's ICT response and recovery plans should be concise and accessible to those with responsibilities defined in the plans. Plans should contain the elements discussed in the following sections.

Purpose and scope

The purpose and scope of each specific plan should be defined, agreed upon by management and understood by those who will invoke the plan. Any relationship to other relevant plans or documents within the organization, particularly to BCPs, should be clearly referenced, and the method of obtaining and accessing these plans should be described.

Each incident management and ICT response and recovery plan should establish prioritized objectives in terms of the following:

•   The critical ICT services to be recovered.
•   The time frame in which they are to be recovered.
•   The recovery level needed for each critical ICT service activity.
•   The situation in which each plan can be invoked.

Plans may also contain, where appropriate, procedures and checklists that support the post-incident review process.

Roles and responsibilities

The roles and responsibilities of the people and teams with authority, in terms of both decision-making and authority to spend during and following an incident, should be clearly documented.

Plan invocation

Invariably, time lost during a response cannot be regained. It is almost always better to initiate an ICT response and subsequently stand it down than to miss an opportunity to contain an incident early and prevent escalation. Therefore, the organization should use the incident management escalation and invocation protocols contained within its wider business continuity incident management plans as the basis for managing potential ICT-related service disruptions. The method by which an ICT response and recovery plan is invoked should be clearly documented. This process should allow for the relevant plans or parts thereof to be invoked in the shortest possible time, either in advance of a potentially disruptive event or immediately after the occurrence of an event. The plan should include clear and precise descriptions of the following:

- How to mobilize the assigned individual or team.
- Immediate rendezvous points.
- Subsequent team meeting locations and details of any alternative meeting locations.
- Circumstances under which an IRBC response is deemed unnecessary— that is, minor faults and outages that, even in the case of critical ICT services, may be managed by normal helpdesk and support arrangements and agreements.
- Process for standing down the ICT response team once the incident is over and returning to business as usual.
- ICT response and recovery plan documentation owner.
- How the owner of the ICT response and recovery plan documentation will be held accountable for regularly reviewing and updating the documentation.
- How a system of version control will be employed, all interested parties formally notified and a formal continuity plan document distribution record maintained.
- Contact details.

ICT response and recovery plan documentation

The ICT response and recovery plan documentation should

- be flexible, feasible and relevant;
- be easy to read and understand; and
- provide a basis for managing serious issues that are deemed to merit an IRBC response, typically following a significant disruption event.

The documentation should define the overarching framework within which the recovery plans are organized, covering the following:

- Overall strategy.
- Critical services with RTOs/RPOs.
- Timelines for recovery.
- Recovery teams and their responsibilities.

The plans should be documented such that competent personnel can use them in the event of an incident and include the following:

- Objectives: A short description of the objectives of the plans.
- Scope: Covering the following, with reference to the results of the BIA:
    - The criticality of services: Description of the relevant services and identification of their criticality.
    - Technology: An overview of the main technology that supports services, including where it is maintained.
    - Business units: An overview of the entities that manage the technology.
    - Documentation: An overview of the main documentation for the technology, including the locations where it is stored.
- Availability requirements: Business-defined requirements for the availability of services and related technology.
- Information security requirements: Requirements for the information security of services, systems and data, including confidentiality, integrity and availability requirements.
- Technology recovery procedures: Description of the procedures to be followed to recover ICT services, including the following:
    - A list of activities—that is, desktop support and restoration contact information.
    - A list of activities for recovering networks, systems, applications and databases to an agreed-upon level at an alternative location, considering the changed environment—that is, how it could affect line capacity and system-to-system communications.
    - A list of activities for restoring basic functionality, such as security, routing and logging.
    - Coordination within the application or among applications, data synchronization and potential automated procedures for handling a backlog of information.
    - The process needed to restore ICT services and turn them over to their users to operate in recovery mode.
    - Backup procedures.
    - Where and how people can obtain further information and instructions—that is, hotline numbers and steps to return to normal.
- Appendices
    - Inventory of information systems, applications and databases.
    - Overview of network infrastructure and server names.
    - Inventory of hardware and systems software.
    - Contracts and service-level agreements (SLAs).

- Key ICT suppliers
  - Business-as-usual suppliers.
  - Recovery service suppliers.

Awareness, competency and training programme

A coordinated programme should be implemented to ensure that processes are in place to regularly promote IRBC awareness in general and to assess and enhance the competency of all personnel who are relevant to the successful implementation of IRBC.

Document control

Control of IRBC records

Controls should be established over IRBC records to

- ensure that they remain legible, readily identifiable and retrievable and
- provide for their storage, protection and retrieval.

Control of IRBC documentation

Controls should be established over IRBC documentation to ensure that

- documents are approved prior to issuance;
- documents are reviewed, updated and re-approved as needed;
- changes and the current revision status of documents are identified;
- relevant versions of applicable documents are available at points of use;
- documents of external origin are identified, and their distribution is controlled; and
- the unintended use of obsolete documents is prevented, and such documents are suitably identified if they are retained for any purpose.

Monitoring and review

Maintaining IRBC

With change comes risk—not only the risk of failure but also the risk of destabilizing existing policies and strategies. IRBC strategies should therefore be resilient and adaptable. Any change to ICT services that may affect

IRBC capability should be implemented only after the business continuity implications of the change have been assessed and addressed.

The following steps are necessary to ensure that the IRBC strategies and plans remain appropriate for the organization:

- Management should ensure that the IRBC strategies continue to support the organization's BCM requirements.
- The change management process should include all parties responsible for the planning and implementation of IRBC strategies.
- The development process for new ICT services should include sign-off that resilience has not been compromised by even the simplest upgrades or improvements.
- Due diligence on merger and acquisition activity should include a resilience assessment.
- ICT component decommissioning should be reflected within related IRBC management systems.

Monitoring, detection and analysis of threats

The organization should establish a process to continuously monitor and detect the emergence of ICT security threats, including but not limited to the following areas:

- Retention of staff, skills and knowledge.
- Management of facilities to house ICT equipment—that is, by monitoring the amount and nature of security.
- Incidents/vulnerabilities related to computer rooms.
- Changes in supporting technology, plants, equipment and networks.
- Changes in information applications and databases.
- Finance or budget allocation.
- The effectiveness of external services and suppliers.

Testing and exercising

The organization should test not only the recovery of the ICT service but also the protection and resilience elements to determine whether

- the service can be protected, maintained and/or recovered regardless of the incident severity,
- the IRBC management arrangements can minimize the impact on the business and
- the procedures for returning to business as usual are valid.

Test and exercise programme

In most instances, the whole set of IRBC elements and processes, including ICT recovery, cannot be proved in one test and exercise.

A progressive exercising regime might therefore be appropriate for building a full simulation of a real incident. The programme should include different levels of exercise, from familiarization to computer room resilience, and should consider all aspects of end-to-end ICT service delivery.

There are risks associated with tests and exercises, and such activities should not expose the organization to an unacceptable level of risk. The test and exercise programme should define how the risk of individual exercising is addressed. Management sign-off on the programme should be obtained, and a clear explanation of the associated risks should be documented.

The test and exercise programme objectives should be fully aligned with the wider BCM scope and objectives and should complement the organization's broader exercise programme. Each test and exercise should have both business objectives, even where there is no direct business involvement, and a defined technical objective to test or validate a specific element of the IRBC strategy.

Exercising individual elements in isolation at the component level is complementary to full system exercising and should be maintained as part of an ongoing test and exercise programme.

The test and exercise programme should define the frequency, scope and format of each exercise. The following are high-level examples of exercise scope:

- Recovery of a single data file or database following corruption.
- Recovery of a single server, including a full rebuild.
- Recovery of an application, which may consist of several servers, sub-applications and infrastructure.
- Failover of services hosted on a high-availability platform—that is, clustering simulating the loss of any member of a cluster.
- Data recovery from tape—that is, recovery of single files or series of files from offsite tape storage.
- Network testing.
- Communications infrastructure failover tests.

Exercises should be progressive to include an increasing test of dependencies and interrelationships and relevant end-user communities.

The scope of exercise

Exercising should be carried out to

- build confidence throughout the organization that the resilience and recovery strategy will meet the business requirements;
- demonstrate that critical ICT services can be maintained and recovered within agreed-upon service levels or recovery objectives regardless of the incident;
- demonstrate that the critical ICT services can be restored to the pre-test state in the event of an incident at the recovery location;
- provide the opportunity for staff to familiarize themselves with the recovery process;
- train staff and ensure that they have adequate knowledge of IRBC plans and procedures;
- check that IRBC remains synchronized with ICT infrastructure and general infrastructure;
- identify any improvements required for the IRBC strategy, architecture or recovery processes; and
- provide evidence for audit purposes and demonstrate the organization's ICT service competence.

Exercising should apply to the entire ICT environment and all the components that deliver end-to-end service, from the computer room through the user desktop or any other service delivery channel.

Elements of service recovery

The organization should exercise all elements of the ICT service recovery as appropriate for its size, complexity and BCM scope. The exercise should not focus solely on service recovery and resumption but should include the reliability of resilience capability, system monitoring and alert management. The organization should exercise from the component level through full location-based system testing to achieve high levels of confidence and resilience.

The following elements should be exercised:

- Computer rooms: Physical security, fire and water leak detection systems and evacuation processes.
- Heating, ventilation and air conditioning; environmental monitoring and alert protocols and electrical services.
- Infrastructure, including the overall resilience of the network connectivity and network diversity.

- Network security, including anti-virus protection and intrusion prevention and detection.
- Hardware, including servers, telecoms equipment, storage arrays and removable media.
- Software.
- Data.
- Services.
- Role and response of suppliers.

Planning an exercise

To ensure that an exercise does not cause incidents or undermine service capability, it should be carefully planned to minimize the risk of an incident occurring as a direct result. This risk management—that is, the elements of service recovery—should be appropriate to the level of the exercise being undertaken. This may include the following:

- Ensuring that all data are backed up immediately prior to the exercise.
- Conducting exercises in isolated environments.
- Scheduling exercises "out of hours" or during quiet times in the business cycle, with knowledge of the end users' primary and secondary desktop process recovery simulation.

Exercises should be realistic, carefully planned and agreed upon with stakeholders so that there is minimum risk of disruption to business processes. The scale and complexity of exercises should be appropriate to the organization's recovery objectives.

Each exercise should have "terms of reference", agreed upon and signed off in advance by the exercise sponsor, which may include the following:

- Description.
- Objectives.
- Scope.
- Assumptions.
- Constraints.
- Risks.
- Success criteria.
- Resources.
- Roles and responsibilities.
- High-level timeline/schedule.
- Exercise data capture.
- Exercise/incident logging.

- Debriefing.
- Post-exercise actions, follow-up and reporting.

An exercise should be planned to enable the organization to achieve the success criteria identified.

Managing an exercise

A clear exercise command structure should be developed, with roles and responsibilities allocated to appropriate individuals. The exercise command structure may include the following:

- Exercise commander and participant(s) with overall control of the test and exercise.
- Exercise communications.
- Confirmation that there are enough staff available to safely undertake the exercise.
- Sufficient observers and/or facilitators to capture the exercise proceedings and maintain an issue log.
- Key exercise milestones.
- End-of-exercise protocols.
- Emergency stop exercise protocols.

The exercise command should ensure the following:

- Objectives and key milestones are met.
- All exercise material and activities have appropriate levels of confidentiality.
- Any ongoing risks are monitored and mitigated.
- Any visitors/observers are authorized.
- The exercise proceedings are captured in a consistent manner.
- All participants are debriefed, and feedback is collated.

Verifying, reviewing and evaluating information security continuity

The organization should verify the established and implemented information security continuity controls at regular intervals to ensure that they are valid and effective during adverse situations. Organizational, technical, procedural and process changes, whether in an operational or continuity context, can lead to changes in information security continuity requirements. In such cases, the continuity of processes, procedures and controls for information security should be reviewed against the changed requirements.

An organization should verify its information security management continuity by

- exercising and testing the functionality of information security continuity processes, procedures and controls to ensure that they are consistent with the information security continuity objectives;
- exercising and testing knowledge and routines to operate information security continuity processes, procedures and controls to ensure that their performance is consistent with the information security continuity objectives; and
- reviewing the validity and effectiveness of information security continuity measures when information systems, information security processes, procedures and controls or BCM/DR management processes and solutions change.

Reviewing, reporting and follow-up

At the end of an exercise, the findings should be reviewed and followed up promptly. This should include the following:

- Gathering the results and findings.
- Analysing the results and findings in relation to the exercise objectives and success criteria.
- Identifying any gaps.
- Assigning action points with defined timelines.
- Creating an exercise report for formal consideration by the exercise sponsor.
- Consolidating and following up on exercise report actions.

IRBC internal audit

The IRBC internal audit plan should define and document the audit criteria, scope, method and frequency, and IRBC internal auditing should be conducted annually. The audit plan should ensure that only qualified internal auditors are appointed to perform the audit. The selection of auditors and the performance of the audit should ensure objectivity and impartiality in the audit process. Auditors conducting IRBC internal audits should be competent to undertake the task. For example, they should undergo relevant auditor training to acquire the necessary skills and knowledge.

A procedure should be established to ensure that deficiencies identified in IRBC internal audits are rectified. The audit plan should also encompass external parties.

For example, outsourcing vendors should be audited for their capability to support the organization's IRBC strategies and plans during daily operation and response to and recovery from disaster.

An internal audit should be conducted when there are significant changes to critical ICT services or business continuity requirements that are relevant to the IRBC scope or IRBC requirements.

The results of the IRBC internal audit should be recorded and reported. Management should review the results of IRBC internal audits and the statuses of follow-up corrective actions.

Management review

Management should ensure that the IRBC management system is reviewed at planned intervals. This review may be based on the input of internal or external audits or self-assessments. The review should include assessing opportunities for improvement and the need for changes to IRBC management, including IRBC policy and objectives. In addition, management should annually review the agreed-upon IRBC requirements, including ICT service definitions, the documented list of critical ICT services and the risks associated with identified gaps between critical ICT readiness capability and business continuity requirements. The results of the review should be clearly documented, and records should be maintained.

Review input

The input to a management review should include information on the following:

- Internal service levels.
- External service providers' ability to maintain appropriate levels of service.
- The results of relevant audits.
- Feedback from interested parties, including independent observations.
- Status of preventative and corrective actions.
- Level of residual risk and acceptable risk.
- Follow-up actions from previous management reviews and recommendations.
- Lessons learned from tests and exercises, incidents, education and awareness programmes and emerging best practices and guidelines.

Review output

The output from the review should be signed off by management and include the following:

- Varying the scope of the IRBC management system.
- Improving the effectiveness of the IRBC management system.
- Revised IRBC requirements, including ICT service definitions, the documented list of critical ICT services and the risks associated with gaps identified between critical ICT readiness capability and business continuity requirements.
- Modifying the IRBC strategy and procedures, as necessary, to respond to internal and/or external events that could impact ICT services, including changes to

  - business requirements,
  - resilience requirements and
  - levels of risk and/or levels of risk acceptance.

- Resource needs.
- Funding and budget requirements.

Measurement of ICT readiness performance criteria

The organization should monitor and measure its ICT readiness through the implementation of the measurement process of the defined ICT readiness performance criteria.

Quantitative and qualitative performance criteria

The performance criteria for IRBC may be qualitative or quantitative. Quantitative criteria may include the following:

- Over a given period, the number of incidents that have not been detected prior to disruption.
- Detection time for incidents.
- Number of incidents that cannot be effectively contained to reduce impact.
- Availability of data sources to indicate the emergence of incidents through trend monitoring of events.
- Time to react and respond to detected emerging incidents.

Qualitative criteria are subjective in determining the performance of IRBC but usually require fewer resources in the measurement process. They may include determining the efficiency of the processes used to plan, prepare and execute IRBC activities and can be measured through

- a survey using a structured or unstructured questionnaire,
- feedback from participants and stakeholders,
- feedback workshops and
- other focused group meetings.

IRBC improvement

The organization should continually improve IRBC through the application of preventative and corrective actions that are appropriate to the potential impacts determined by its BIA and risk appetite.

Corrective action

The organization should take action to correct any actual failure of the ICT service and elements of IRBC. The documented procedure for corrective action should define requirements for

- identifying failures,
- determining the causes of failures,
- evaluating the need for actions to avoid non-conformities,
- determining and implementing the corrective action needed,
- recording the results of action taken and
- reviewing corrective action taken.

Preventative action

The organization should identify potential weaknesses in the elements of IRBC and establish documented procedures for

- identifying potential failures,
- identifying the causes of failures,
- determining and implementing the preventative action needed and
- recording and reviewing the results of action taken.

7 Cybersecurity risk-management framework

Cyber risk investment model

The cyber risk investment model is composed of the following elements:

1   Technology landscape.
2   Data classification.
3   Risk-management practices.
4   Cost–benefit analysis for cybersecurity measures.
5   Business objectives.

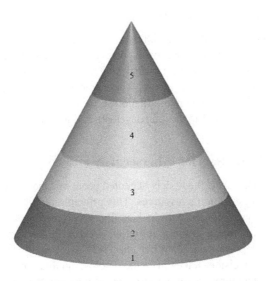

Figure 7.1 The cyber risk investment model, which comprises the (1) technology landscape and application portfolio, (2) data-centric focus, (3) risk-management practices, (4) cost–benefit analysis and (5) strategic development (Kissoon, 2020).

DOI: 10.4324/9781003200895-7

Technology landscape

The technology landscape is defined as the technology and information security measures in place within the enterprise architecture. This landscape is usually depicted through enterprise architecture artefacts that include but are not limited to the visual layout of the technology, system interfaces, communication channels, application portfolios, technology stack and security measures. This landscape extends from the on-premises environment to suppliers, service providers, agents and partners.

Data classification

Data classification, in the context of cyber risk management, is the classification of data based on their level of impact on an organization and includes collection, use, disclosure and retention. The protection of data is based on the data classification level—that is, public, internal use, confidential or restricted. These levels define the type of safeguards that should be in place to adequately protect the data, regardless of how they are stored. Protection of data includes safeguards to minimize loss, theft, unauthorized access, use, disclosure, copying and modification.

Risk-management practices

All organizations are confronted with risks that have the potential to negatively affect their business. Risk-management practices in the financial services sector focus on identifying, measuring and analysing those threats to reduce material, reputation, opportunity and other costs. These practices utilize the ERM framework, which is integrated with information security, privacy risk, vulnerability management, system and application development lifecycles along with BCM.

Cost–benefit analysis for cybersecurity measures

Cost–benefit analysis is the widely accepted economic principle for managing all of an organization's resources. This principle requires that the costs of an activity be compared with its benefits. When the benefits exceed the costs, it pays to engage in those activities, whereas if the costs exceed the benefits, the opposite is true. When the costs and benefits of an activity are equal, the decision-maker may factor other qualitative measures into the decision. The three major activities usually associated with cybersecurity are (1) protecting information from authorized users of the information, (2) making information available to authorized users on a timely basis and (3) protecting information from integrity flaws.

Business objectives

Business objectives are specific and measurable goals that an organization wants to attain as it focuses on growth, profitability, efficiency and stability. These objectives are interconnected with the enterprise strategy and appear directly within the business strategy and multi-year road map.

Cybersecurity risk-management framework

Risk signifies an uncertain event that may occur in a present or future process and *can* affect elements within the process. In the context of software engineering, some additional definitions are useful. Risk is defined as a two-part function: (1) the adverse impact an event would have if it occurred and (2) the likelihood of the event occurring.

To further understand risk, it is essential to understand what is considered an adverse event. These unfavourable events can be viewed from multiple levels of abstraction and can occur in different stages of maturity. The maturity level is often categorized as one of the following three types: failures, errors and bugs. These terms are often erroneously believed to be interchangeable, but in the scope of risk management and software testing, they carry significantly different meanings.

- A failure is a malfunction of the programme in relation to specifications and/or expected behaviour.
- An error is the state of the programme in which failures occur.
- A fault is the root cause in the codebase or environment of the error state and is used interchangeably with the term "bug".

The aim of risk management is for an organization to implement a framework that covers the work related to the risk associated with its environment. The goal is to continuously identify, analyse and assess the risk associated with the organization in a systematic, procedural manner. Risk management can, in many cases, assist in mitigating the risk of adverse events and prepare responses for a situation in which one or several identified risks have occurred. A significant amount of research has been dedicated to standardizing risk-management methodologies, both in the scope of software projects and in more general terms. One study that is often referenced is the National Institute of Standards and Technology (NIST) SP 800–39 Risk-Management Process, which states that core activities should take place in an organization's risk-management process to ensure that it is sufficient. These activities are outlined as follows:

1 Framing risk is the step where the context of the risk is defined and the potential risk factors are identified.

2   Assessing risk is the step where the probability and potential impact of a risk factor are examined.

3   Responding to risk is the step where decisions are made regarding how to react to an adverse event and what to make of the assessed risk factors.

4   Identifying risk has no inherent value; mitigating negative value through response plans and risk avoidance is what results in value.

5   Monitoring risk is the process of monitoring the implementation and effectiveness of the risk-management plan determined through the other steps. This step is the continuous aspect of risk management and is responsible for identifying new risks, developing more efficient solutions and tracking.

Risk assessment is an essential part of any organizational process—that is, business, technology and software—and can involve external third parties, such as suppliers, agents and vendors. There are many different definitions, but at its most basic, it is the process of gathering information related to the process or processes of interest to assess the risks related to them. It often includes estimating both the likelihood that an event will negatively affect the organization—that is, processes, technology and projects—and the extent to which that adversity will impact the organization. It is a complex process that requires analysing the relevant data related to the specific processes, technologies and projects, as well as the data related to the organization and potential end users.

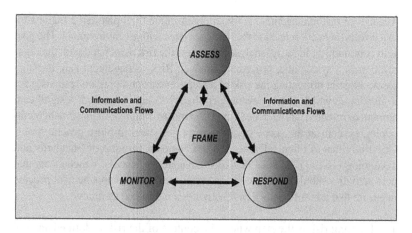

Figure 7.2 The elements of the risk-management process (NIST, 2020).

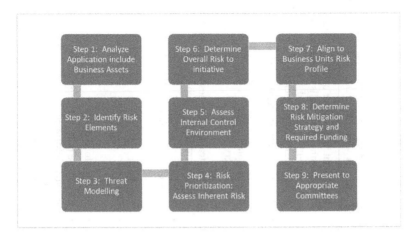

Figure 7.3 The digital cybersecurity risk-management assessment process (Kissoon, 2020).

Risk-assessment process

The risk-assessment process identifies critical risk elements, and some examples are as follows:

1 Data classification.
2 Strategic/business requirements.
3 Application development.
4 Vendor relationships.
5 Technology landscape.
6 Legal/regulatory issues.
7 Brand/reputational issues.
8 Operational issues.
9 Financial issues.
10 Security and fraud issues.

Threat modelling

Threat modelling enables threats and their means of mitigation to be identified, communicated and understood within the context of protecting something of value. Threat modelling can be applied to a wide range of items, including software, applications, systems, networks, distributed systems,

Table 7.1 A sample threat risk assessment (Kissoon, 2020).

Threat		Risk Level	Mitigation	Mitigation in Microsoft Teams
Spoofing: process, machine, person	Impersonation	High	Access control authentication	• Implement multi-factor authentication (MFA) using phone calls or text messages • One-time-use password • Conditional access policies
Tampering: process, memory	Malicious code	High	Integrity permissions	• Advance threat protection (ATP)
Repudiation: process, person	Impersonation	High	Accountability Fraud prevention Logging Signatures	• Information barriers • E-discovery: logging, retention: team chats, messaging, integration with MS stream for video
Information disclosure in process	Malicious code Data leakage	High	Confidentiality Permissions Encryption	• Safe links • Data loss prevention (DLP)
Information disclosure: data stores, data flows	Phishing Data leakage	High	Confidentiality Permissions Encryption	• Safe links • DLP
Denial of service	Sabotage	High	Availability	• Review cloud design
Elevation of privileges	Impersonation	High	Access control Authorization Isolation	• Customize policy setting: sharing of sensitive information • Information barriers

Table 7.2 A sample threat risk assessment (Kissoon, 2020).

What Can Go Wrong?	Threat Type	Mitigation
1 Lack of a user access management process with appropriate management approval	Authentication	1 An approved user (AU) access management process is in place.
2 Creation of unauthorized administrator/administrator-equivalent accounts		2 Credentials and authentication mechanisms are protected with encryption in storage and transit.
		3 Protocols are resistant to brute force, dictionary and replay attacks.
		4 Strong password policies are enforced.
		5 Trusted server authentication is used instead of SQL authentication.
		6 Passwords are stored with salted hashes.
3 Creation of rogue accounts		7 Password resets do not reveal password hints or valid usernames.
		8 Account lockouts do not result in a denial-of-service attack.
		9 Auditing and logging of all administration activities are enabled.
4 Misuse of administrator/administrator-equivalent accounts	Authorization	1 Strong access control lists (ACLs) are used to enforce authorized access to resources.
		2 Role-based access controls are used to restrict access to specific operations.
		3 The system follows the principle of least privilege for user and service accounts.
5 Misuse of rogue accounts		4 Privilege separation is correctly configured within the presentation, business and data access layers.
6 Injection of malicious code		5 Auditing and logging of all administration activities are enabled.
7 Alteration of current configuration settings	Configuration management	1 Least privileged processes are used, and service accounts have no administration capability.
		2 Auditing and logging of all administration activities are enabled.
8 Ability to launch phishing attacks		3 Access to configuration files and administrator interfaces is restricted to administrators.
9 Disclosure of information	Data protection in storage and transit	1 Standard encryption algorithms and correct key sizes are used.
		2 Hashed message authentication codes (HMACs) are used to protect data integrity.
		3 Secrets (i.e., keys, confidential data) are cryptographically protected both in transport and in storage.
		4 Built-in secure storage is used to protect keys.
		5 No credentials or sensitive data are sent in clear text.

(Continued)

Table 7.2 (Continued)

What Can Go Wrong?	Threat Type	Mitigation	
10	Alteration of application code	Data validation/ parameter validation	1	Data type, format, length and range checks are enforced.
			2	All data sent from the client are validated.
			3	No security decision is based upon parameters (e.g., URL parameters) that can be manipulated.
			4	Input filtering via whitelist validation is used.
			5	Output encoding is used.
11	Ability to disrupt the application	Error handling and exception management	1	All exceptions are handled in a structured manner.
			2	Privileges are restored to the appropriate level in case of errors and exceptions.
			3	Error messages are scrubbed to ensure that no sensitive information is revealed to the attacker.
12	Leakage of sensitive information	User and session management	1	No sensitive information is stored in clear text in the cookie.
			2	The content of the authentication cookies is encrypted.
			3	Cookies are configured to expire.
			4	Sessions are resistant to replay attacks.
			5	Secure communication channels are used to protect authentication cookies.
			6	The user is forced to re-authenticate when performing critical functions.
			7	Sessions expire at logout.
13	Malicious activity goes unnoticed	Auditing and logging	1	Sensitive information (e.g., passwords, PII) is not logged.
			2	Access controls (e.g., ACLs) are enforced on log files to prevent unauthorized access.
			3	Integrity controls (e.g., signatures) are enforced on log files to provide non-repudiation.
			4	Log files provide an audit trail for sensitive operations and logging of key events.
			5	Auditing and logging are enabled across tiers on multiple servers.

the Internet of Things and business processes. One methodology for identifying and classifying threats is STRIDE, which can be an effective way to understand threats that place business assets at risk.

Example: Threat Risk Assessment—Microsoft Teams is built on the Office 365 hyper-scale enterprise-grade cloud and delivers the following security and compliance capabilities.

Vulnerability: Anonymous individuals can connect to Microsoft Teams using a guest account.

Risk prioritization: Assess the inherent risk

The risk-assessment process is based on a questionnaire in which a set of questions is formulated for each risk element. Examples of the question categories include the following:

- Financial loss.
- Media attention.
- Reportable to regulator.
- Impact on suppliers and employees.
- Loss or damage to information systems with very limited downtime.

Each question can be answered in one of five ways, in increasing order of risk, such that a risk score between 1 and 5 can be assigned for that question based on two rating scales—that is, likelihood and impact. A quantitative inherent risk score can be calculated for each question, each risk element and the overall project, as follows:

- Risk score per question: Product of the likelihood and impact rating.
- Risk score per element: Accumulating the numerical score per question and dividing it by the number of questions for a risk element.
- Risk score for the overall initiative: Accumulating the numerical score per risk element and dividing it by the number of risk elements in each project.

This quantitative inherent risk score is assigned a qualitative risk score categorized as high, medium or low. The qualitative inherent risk score shows which element carries the most risk, making it easier for decision-makers to decide where to allocate resources.

Impact rating scale

Table 7.3 shows the quantitative scale for the impact rating based on a score of 1–5.

Table 7.3 A sample impact rating scale (Kissoon, 2020).

Impact	Criteria
Critical **5**	• Financial loss of over $5 million. • International short-term negative media coverage with impact on market share. • Reportable to regulator and requires a corrective action plan and implementation dates. • Legal and regulatory impact to include the following: fees, fines, litigation, compliance enforcement and senior executive impact. • Significant impact on suppliers and employees. • Significant loss or permanent damage to information systems, excessive downtime, over triple the expected RTO.
Major **4**	• Financial loss of $1 million up to $5 million. • National short-term negative media coverage, potential to lose market share. • Reportable to regulator and requires a corrective action plan. • Some senior managers are impacted. • Impact on suppliers and employees. • Major loss or damage to information systems, continuous downtime, increase to expected RTO.
Moderate **3**	• Financial loss of $500,00 up to $1 million • Short-term negative media coverage • Reportable to regulator with a potential of corrective plan to be provided • Minimal impact to suppliers and employees • Some loss or damage to information systems, intermittent downtime, possible to achieve expected RTO
Minor **2**	• Financial loss of $100,000 up to $500,000. • No reputational damage. • No media attention. • No reportable incident to regulator. • Minimal impact to suppliers and employees. • Minimal loss or damage to information systems with minimal downtime.
Insignificant **1**	• Financial loss up to $100,000. • No media attention. • Not reportable to regulator. • No impact on suppliers and employees. • No significant loss or damage to information systems with very limited downtime.

Likelihood rating scale

Table 7.4 shows the quantitative scale for the impact rating based on a score of 1–5.

Table 7.4 A sample likelihood rating scale (Kissoon, 2020).

Likelihood	Criteria
Almost Certain **5**	• Almost certain. • Minimum of once in 6 months. • Greater than 90% chance of occurrence over the life of the asset or project.
Likely **4**	• Likely. • Minimum of once in 1 year. • 60% to 90% chance of occurrence over the life of the asset or project.
Possible **3**	• Possible. • Minimum of once in 5 years. • 30% to 60% chance of occurrence over the life of the asset or project.
Unlikely **2**	• Unlikely. • Minimum of once in 10 years. • 10% to 30% chance of occurrence over the life of the asset or project.
Rare **1**	• Rare. • Minimum of once in 20 years. • <10% chance of occurrence over the life of the asset or project.

Qualitative inherent risk rating

Table 7.5 shows the scale of the qualitative inherent risk rating based on the quantitative inherent risk score.

Table 7.5 A sample qualitative inherent risk rating scale (Kissoon, 2020).

Inherent Risk	Quantitative Risk Calculation
High	Range: 10+
Medium	Range: 4–10
Low	Range: 1–4

Assess the internal controls

Internal control environment

The control environment and monitoring activities are foundational for an organization to effectively manage its information security risk exposure. As stated in the *2013 COSO Framework*,

> The control environment is the set of standards, processes, and structures that provide the basis for carrying out internal control across the organization. The board of directors and senior management establish the tone at the top regarding the importance of internal control and expected standards of conduct.

Cybersecurity and privacy risk framework

The privacy framework approach to privacy risk involves considering privacy events as potential problems individuals could experience that arise from system, product or service operations with data, whether in digital or non-digital form, through a complete lifecycle from data collection through disposal.

Privacy framework functions

The five privacy framework functions are defined in the following sections.

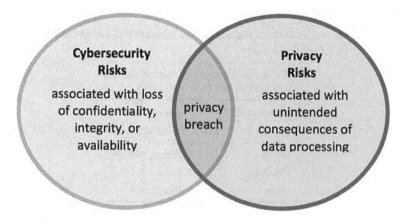

Figure 7.4 A cybersecurity and privacy risk relationship (NIST, 2020).

IDENTIFY-P

Identify-P develops the organization's understanding of how to manage privacy risks for individuals arising from data processing. The activities in the identify-P function are foundational for the effective use of the privacy framework. Inventorying the circumstances under which data are processed, understanding the privacy interests of individuals who are directly or indirectly served or affected by the organization and conducting risk assessments enable an organization to understand the business environment in which it is operating and identifies and prioritizes privacy risks.

GOVERN-P

Govern-P develops and implements an organization's governance structure to enable an ongoing understanding of the risk-management priorities that are informed by privacy risk. The govern-P function is similarly foundational but focuses on organization-level activities—for example, (1) establishing the organization's privacy values and policies, (2) identifying legal/regulatory requirements and (3) understanding the risk tolerance that enables the organization to focus and prioritize its efforts in ways that are consistent with its risk-management strategy and business needs.

CONTROL-P

Control-P develops and implements appropriate activities to enable the organization to manage data with sufficient granularity to understand privacy risks. The control-P function is associated with data processing management from the perspectives of both organizations and individuals.

PROTECT P

Protect-P develops and implements appropriate data processing safeguards. The protect-P function covers data protection to prevent cybersecurity-related privacy events and represents the intersection of privacy and cybersecurity risk management.

COMMUNICATE-P

Communicate-P develops and implements appropriate activities to enable the organization to have a reliable understanding of how data are processed and the associated privacy risks.

The communicate-P function includes the recognition that both the organization and individuals may need to know how data are processed to effectively manage privacy risks.

Privacy risk assessments

Privacy risk management is a cross-organizational set of processes that assist the organization in understanding how its systems, products and services may create concerns for individuals and how to develop effective solutions to manage these risks. *Privacy risk assessment* is a sub-process of identifying and evaluating specific privacy risks. In general, privacy risk assessments produce information that can assist organizations in weighing the benefits of data processing against the risks to determine the appropriate response.

The internal control environment is defined as the technology and information security controls in place within the enterprise architecture. This landscape is usually depicted through enterprise architecture artefacts, which include but are not limited to diagrams, interfaces, communication channels and application/technology portfolios. In addition, it extends from the on-premises environment to suppliers, service providers, agents and partners. Therefore, in addition to internal assessments, external third-party assurance reports are utilized to assist with internal control environment assessments.

Cybersecurity framework

Some organizations utilize cybersecurity risk-based frameworks to manage cybersecurity risk. The industry framework has been established through NIST and is composed of the following three parts: the framework core, the framework implementation tiers and the framework profiles. Each framework component strengthens the integration between cybersecurity activities and business drivers.

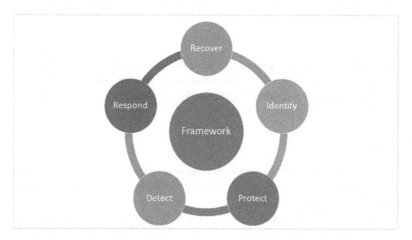

Figure 7.5 The NIST cybersecurity framework (NIST, 2020).

The framework core is a set of cybersecurity activities, desired outcomes and applicable references that are common across critical infrastructure sectors. The core provides industry standards, guidelines and practices in a way that allows the communication of cybersecurity activities and outcomes from the executive level to the implementation/operations level.

The framework core consists of five concurrent and continuous functions—identify, protect, detect, respond and recover. When considered as a whole, these functions provide a high-level strategic perspective on the lifecycle of an organization's management of cybersecurity risk through an assessment of the internal control environment. The framework core then identifies the underlying key categories and subcategories of the specific outcomes for each function. These outcomes are equated with informative references, such as existing standards, guidelines and practices, for each subcategory.

Vendor assurance reports

As outsourcing service providers (OSPs) manage a significant amount of customer data, systems, processes and operations, their ability to manage associated risks while meeting increasing compliance requirements often emerges as a priority. Many service providers are reactive to third-party reporting due to the lack of full visibility in their reporting portfolios. Creating a library of enterprise-wide requirements and mapping individual obligations to corresponding controls can help identify gaps and overlaps. For example, an organization may have one control for regulating physical access to its data centre, but it may align with 20 different internal and external requirements. An integrated library of requirements and control tests can make it easier to compile customer-centric reports.

Outsourcing is a growing trend, and companies increasingly depend on third-party providers to deliver critical services. The purpose of third-party reports—that is, SOC2 or ISAE3402 reviews—is to provide client auditors with an objective report that expresses an opinion about the control environment of a service organization. These reports are designed to provide assurances about the effectiveness of the controls in place at a service organization—that is, SOC for Service Organizations: Trust Services Criteria (SOC2) assesses the security, availability or processing integrity of the system used to process client information or the confidentiality or privacy of that information.

Determine the organizational risk appetite

An organization's risk appetite is the amount of risk, on a broad level, that an organization is willing to accept as it attempts to achieve its goals and provide value to its stakeholders.

Table 7.6 A sample residual risk rating scale (Optiv, 2011).

		Inherent Risk		
		Low	Medium	High
Control effectiveness	Highly effective	Low	Low	Medium–low
	Effective	Low	Medium–low	Medium
	Partially effective	Low	Medium–low	Medium–high
	Ineffective	Low	Medium	High
		Low	Medium	High
		Residual risk		

During the risk-assessment process, an organization's residual risk is assessed to determine the remaining risk after internal controls are implemented.

Assessing this risk shows the organization the areas where a gap or lack of internal control exists. Usually, this is the area of focus for key stakeholders as they perform the cost–benefit analysis and determine the risk-mitigation strategy. In essence, residual risk should be aligned with the organization's/ business unit's risk profile within the risk tolerance level.

Specifically, the residual risk score is a qualitative score that is more granular than the inherent risk score. The inherent risk is assigned one of three scores—that is, high, medium or low—while the residual risk is commonly assessed based on five or more possible scores—that is, high, medium-high, medium, medium-low and low. This granularity highlights the control implementation progress over time and better reflects changes in the overall risk.

Risk-mitigation strategy

In some circumstances, to align the residual risk with the organization's/ business unit's risk appetite, further mitigation is required. Therefore, organizations are required to make decisions about funding cybersecurity activities in a manner consistent with the viewpoints of various stakeholders. Table 7.7 lists a risk treatment scale that aligns the impact, likelihood and inherent risk rating scale to identify areas that may require governance and risk mitigation through senior management oversight and additional cybersecurity measures.

Cost–benefit analysis is the widely accepted economic principle for managing an organization's resources. This principle requires that the costs of an activity be compared with its benefits. When the benefits exceed the costs, it pays to engage in those activities, whereas if the costs exceed the benefits,

Table 7.7 A sample risk treatment scale (Queensland Treasury and Trade, 2011).

Impact					
Likelihood	Insignificant	Minor	Moderate	Major	Critical
Rare	LOW: accept the risk, routine management	LOW: accept the risk, routine management	LOW: accept the risk, routine management	MEDIUM: specific accountability, risk-mitigation plan	HIGH: quarterly senior management review
Unlikely	LOW: accept the risk, routine management	LOW: accept the risk, routine management	MEDIUM: specific accountability, risk-mitigation plan	MEDIUM: specific accountability, risk-mitigation plan	HIGH: quarterly senior management review
Possible	LOW: accept the risk, routine management	MEDIUM: specific accountability, risk-mitigation plan	MEDIUM: specific accountability, risk-mitigation plan	HIGH: quarterly senior management review	HIGH: quarterly senior management review
Likely	MEDIUM: specific accountability, risk-mitigation plan	MEDIUM: specific accountability, risk-mitigation plan	HIGH: quarterly senior management review	HIGH: quarterly senior management review	EXTREME: monthly senior management review
Almost certain	MEDIUM: specific accountability, risk-mitigation plan	MEDIUM: specific accountability, risk-mitigation plan	HIGH: quarterly senior management review	EXTREME: monthly senior management review	EXTREME: monthly senior management review

the opposite is true. When the costs and benefits of an activity are equal, the decision-maker may factor other qualitative measures into the decision.

The three major activities usually associated with cybersecurity are (1) protecting the information of the authorized users of the information, (2) making information available to the authorized users on a timely basis and (3) protecting information from integrity flaws.

The costs associated with these activities are significant, as organizations will incur costs to detect and correct security breaches that cannot be prevented. The benefits of cybersecurity are related to the cost savings, known as cost avoidance, associated with preventing cybersecurity breaches. The cost–benefit framework states that the goal of an organization should be to implement security procedures up to a point where the benefits minus the costs are maximized. In this framework, implementing cybersecurity activities beyond that point means that the incremental costs are greater than the incremental benefits of the additional security measures. In essence, the net benefit of implementing incremental cybersecurity measures beyond the maximum point is negative and, therefore, represents a financial cost to the organization.

In contrast, the cybersecurity risk-management framework has four areas of consideration: (1) alignment with the organization's risk appetite, (2) alignment with the risk-assessment process, (3) understanding of the cost–benefit analysis and (4) justification of the risk-mitigation strategy. Although cost–benefit analysis is impactful from a financial perspective, in some cases, other factors need to be considered to fully understand the impact of not implementing additional security measures. Incurring the cost of preventative security measures is essential, as in most cost–benefit analyses, the actual cost of remediating a cybersecurity breach is unrealized. Specifically, most organizations do not have the data to appropriately assess the cost/impact of a cybersecurity breach on an organization, such as its effect on the organization's brand/reputation, legal/regulatory landscape, operational/technology environment, forensic/e-discovery-related items and third-party suppliers. Therefore, to adequately implement cybersecurity measures, in addition to conducting a cost–benefit analysis, stakeholders should implement an elaborate decision-making process to determine the additional security measures needed to adequately protect an organization from a cybersecurity breach while aligning with its risk appetite.

8   Case studies

Case study #1 – Möbius solution

Möbius is an industry-leading digital learning platform that excels at creating and deploying interactive teaching and assessment content for higher-educational institutions around the world. Currently, ABC University uses Maple TA, which is a vendor-built, on-premises testing and assessment software solution. The intent of this initiative is to migrate this platform to a software-as-a-service (SAS) version of this solution known as Möbius. The Möbius Platform offers an interactive, online approach for ABC University students interested in pursuing science, technology, engineering and math courses. This initiative will also facilitate integration with the university's learning management system (LMS). The students' information, grades and courses will reside within this application.

Questions

1   Determine the inherent risk.
2   Assess the internal control environment using the NIST Cybersecurity Framework: Core Components.
3   Determine the risk appetite, risk tolerance and risk profile.
4   Assess the residual risk and provide recommendations, if appropriate.
5   Develop the risk-mitigation strategy.

Solution

Business overview

With more than 15 years in the market, the Möbius Platform is used by students, teaching assistants and professors at some of the largest institutions

DOI: 10.4324/9781003200895-8

worldwide. Möbius is a robust online authoring and delivery environment specifically designed to meet the needs of science, technology, engineering and mathematics (STEM) classrooms. It includes a suite of tools and features for authors aiming to design and develop digital assets for their students or peers and a delivery environment that enables and promotes deep and active learning for users through the combination of instructional material and hands-on activities.

The Möbius Platform offers the following:

- A mechanism for creating and deploying online STEM courses.
- Lessons, assessments and interactive learning activities that unfold the potential for STEM students to acquire knowledge at a guided, yet self-defined, pace.
- Complex STEM disciplines with its world-class math engine.
- The ability to create and use powerful multimedia visualizations to anchor key STEM concepts.
- Immediate and meaningful feedback to students and data on student engagement and understanding for instructors.
- Advanced question types with algorithmically generated and randomized questions.
- Access to high-quality content created by curriculum experts.
- Seamless integration with ABC's LMS.

Technical overview

The Möbius Platform is vendor owned by DigitalEd. This cloud-based solution is hosted within the Google Cloud Platform (GCP) System and the Alibaba Cloud.

Risk assessment

IMPACT AND LIKELIHOOD

The impact and likelihood rating scale outlines the evaluation of the protection requirement level for each protection requirement. Table 8.1 shows the impact and likelihood rating as it applies to the risk elements.

INHERENT RISK

The inherent risk has been assigned based on one of three scores of high, medium or low, as shown in Table 8.2.

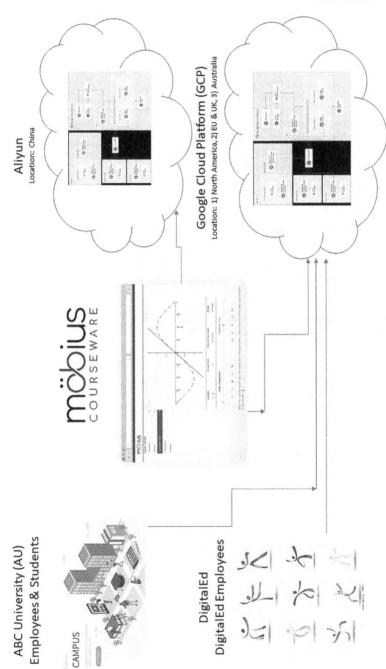

Figure 8.1 The technical overview of the Möbius Platform.

Table 8.1 The impact and likelihood rating scale as applied to the risk elements.

	Risk Element	Impact	Likelihood
1	*Data Classification*	Major	Frequent
	PII: The protection of PII is subject to routine risk-assessment processes. A privacy impact assessment (PIA) is managed by ABC's FOIP office. PII elements are captured and stored through this cloud-hosted web application platform—specifically, any personal information that is used regarding an ABC student to include but not limited to the following:		
	• Student information. • Grades. • Course information. • Connectivity to the Learning Tool Interoperability.		
	Sensitive Authentication Data (SAD): This is the information on a payment card used for authentication at the time of a purchase. This includes data from the full magnetic strip, card security code (CSC, CVV2, CID, CAV2) and personal identification number (PIN). The Möbius Platform facilitates payment card transactions from ABC individuals, so the protection of SAD is required by DigitalEd.		
2	*Business Requirements*	Moderate	Likely
	The Möbius Platform is used within the ABC student environment to provide a comprehensive online courseware platform focusing on the unique needs of STEM students.		
3	*Application Development*	Minor	Possible
	Application development is minimal to include integration with the Möbius Platform. Development includes a standard interface within the university's LMS and connectivity to learning tool interoperability (LTI).		
4	*Vendor Relationship*	Moderate	Likely
	DigitalEd is a privately held Canadian company, with approximately 65 employees worldwide. DigitalEd is an online learning company with a simple and resonant purpose to shape the world through digital learning. DigitalEd introduced the Möbius Platform in spring 2017 with the intent of improving the online learning experiences of authors, instructors and students in STEM-based classrooms.		
5	*Technology Landscape*	Major	Frequent
	Suppliers and third-party partners include the GCP System and Aliyun.		

Risk Element	Impact	Likelihood
6 *Legal/Regulatory*	Major	Possible
Disclosure of data subject to specific regulatory requirements.		
Lawsuits by aggrieved owners of lost or compromised data—that is, PII.		
Fines and penalties assessed by regulators.		
7 *Brand/Reputational*	Minor	Possible
Unflattering or negative publicity due to press coverage that damages ABC's brand.		
Loss of customer confidence due to the release or compromise of data.		
8 *Operational*	Moderate	Likely
Loss of operations and use of the system by authorized users.		
9 *Financial*	Minor	Possible
Significant costs to restore/repair any damages caused by intentional/unintentional users.		
10 *Security and Fraud Issues*	Major	Frequent
Loss and/or manipulation of sensitive data—that is, PII—through disclosure of authentication credentials, DDoS attacks or malware attacks.		

Table 8.2 The inherent risk rating scale as applied to the risk elements.

Risk Element	Quantitative Inherent Risk Rating			Qualitative Inherent Risk Rating
	Impact	Likelihood	Rating	
1 Data classification	4	5	20	High
2 Business requirements	3	4	12	High
3 Application development	2	3	6	Medium
4 Vendor relationship	3	4	12	High
5 Technology landscape	4	5	20	High
6 Legal/regulatory	4	3	12	High
7 Brand/reputational	2	3	6	Medium
8 Operational	3	4	12	High
9 Financial	2	3	6	Medium
10 Security and fraud issues	4	5	20	High
Average			12.6	High

Internal control environment: Effective

The core components of the NIST Cybersecurity Framework were utilized to adequately assess the DigitalEd environment supporting the Möbius Platform. Specifically, the following suppliers and third-party partners provided internal control documentation: (1) Higher Education Community Vendor Assessment Tool (HECVAT)—Lite: DigitalEd, (2) System and Organization Controls (SOC) 2 Type II Report: GCP System for May 1, 2019, to April 30, 2020, period and (3) the Payment Card Industry (PCI) Data Security Standard (DSS) self-assessment questionnaire (SAQ) as of March 21, 2019.

ASSET MANAGEMENT

- Physical devices and systems within suppliers and third-party partners—that is, DigitalEd and Google—are inventoried.
- Software platforms and applications within suppliers and third-party partners—that is, DigitalEd and Google—are inventoried.
- Organizational communication and data flows are mapped.
- External information systems are catalogued.
- Resources—that is, hardware, devices, data, time, personnel and software—are prioritized based on their classification, criticality and business value.
- Cybersecurity roles and responsibilities for the entire workforce and third-party stakeholders—that is, suppliers, customers and partners—are established.
- Google has policies and procedures in place to establish acceptable use of information assets.
- Google has established policies and guidelines to govern data classification, labelling and security.

BUSINESS ENVIRONMENT

- The university's role in the supply chain, critical infrastructure and its industry sector is identified and communicated.
- The priorities for DigitalEd's mission, objectives and activities are established and communicated.
- The dependencies and critical functions for the delivery of critical services are established.
- The resilience requirements to support the delivery of critical services are established for all operating states—that is, under duress/attack—during recovery or under normal operations.

GOVERNANCE

- An organizational cybersecurity policy is established and communicated.
- Cybersecurity roles and responsibilities are coordinated and aligned with internal roles and external partners.
- The legal and regulatory requirements regarding cybersecurity, including privacy and civil liberties obligations, are understood and managed.
- The governance and risk-management processes address cybersecurity risks.
- Google personnel are required to abide by the code of conduct and internal privacy and information security policies.
- Google has established a disciplinary process for non-compliance with the code of conduct, security policy and other personnel requirements, which could include dismissal, lawsuits and/or criminal prosecution.
- Formal organizational structures exist and are available to Google employees on the company's intranet. The intranet provides drill-down functionality for identifying employees on each functional team.
- Each Google team establishes their own standard operating procedures, which are documented and maintained for employees to access.

RISK ASSESSMENT

- Asset vulnerabilities are identified and documented.
- Cyber threat intelligence is received from information-sharing forums and sources.
- Threats, both internal and external, are identified and documented.
- Potential business impacts and likelihoods are identified.
- Threats, vulnerabilities, likelihoods and impacts are used to determine risk.
- Risk responses are identified and prioritized.
- Google developed and maintained a risk-management framework to manage risk to an acceptable level.
- A formal risk assessment is performed by Google annually, at minimum, to determine the likelihood and impact of identified risks using qualitative and quantitative methods. The likelihood and impact associated with each risk are determined independently, considering each risk category.
- Within Google, risks are mitigated to acceptable levels based on the risk criteria, including resolution time frames, which are established, documented and approved by management.

RISK-MANAGEMENT STRATEGY

- Risk-management processes are established, managed and approved by key stakeholders.
- ABC's risk tolerance was determined and clearly expressed.
- ABC's determination of risk tolerance is informed by its role in the critical infrastructure and sector-specific risk analysis.

SUPPLY CHAIN RISK MANAGEMENT

- Cyber supply chain risk-management processes are identified, established, assessed, managed and approved by ABC stakeholders.
- Suppliers and third-party partners of information systems, components and services are identified, prioritized and assessed using a cyber supply chain risk-assessment process.
- Contracts with suppliers and third-party partners are used to implement appropriate measures designed to meet the objectives of an organization's cybersecurity programme and cyber supply chain risk-management plan.
- Suppliers and third-party partners are routinely assessed using audits, test results or other forms of evaluations to confirm that they meet their contractual obligations.
- Response and recovery planning and testing are conducted with suppliers and third-party providers.
- Google has developed policies and procedures that govern third-party relationships.
- Google has agreements with suppliers that include requirements to address information security risks.
- The Google Vendor Security Assessment team takes a risk-based approach to review the security practices of vendors and the security posture of vendor products. Reviews may include automated and manual assessments as determined by the sensitivity of the data being processed or the access being granted.
- Google's sub-processor performance is managed through periodic assessment of the sub-processor control environment.
- Google has an internal audit function and regularly engages third parties to conduct independent reviews of the effectiveness of the organization's approach to managing information security.
- Google has an established internal audit function, which evaluates management's compliance with Google's identity management, source code management and infrastructure controls.
- Google has developed policies and procedures that govern third-party relationships.

- Google has agreements with suppliers that include requirements to address information security risks.

- The Möbius Platform uses roles (Student, Instructor and Administrator) to grant levels of access. These roles are managed at the application tier unless LTI or LDAP is being used, in which case they are mapped from the information provided by these services.
- Software access to hosted instances is granted securely to the Möbius development staff to establish and maintain the software. All access is granted/revoked based on "need to know" best practices. DigitalEd's tools handle access to machines through the enforcement of the public RSA keys that are created by the users needing access. Employees are required to use unique credentials when conducting administrative functions.
- Möbius is fully interactive and provides validation and error messages to help guide the user.
- Each Möbius instance is deployed in its own container on the GCP, and all data are stored in an isolated database.
- To gain access to Möbius, users must register and authenticate with a valid username and password.
- Users of the Möbius service can be authenticated by external LDAP or API services.
- All access, error and system messaging in addition to application logging is enabled. Audit logs contain login, logout, source Internet protocol (IP) addresses and a variety of actions performed.
- All traffic to Möbius traverses a wireless access firewall (WAF). For selected paths, DigitalEd can direct that traffic to the WAF with both standard checks and specific checks for the application. DigitalEd can change the set of paths on demand.
- Software access to hosted instances is granted securely to Möbius development staff to set up and maintain the software. All access is granted/revoked based on "need to know" best practices. The software handles access to machines through enforcement of public RSA keys that are created by the users needing access.
- GCP employs various next-generation threat protection (NGPT) techniques at the data centre level, as outlined here: https://storage.googleapis.com/gfw-touched-accounts-pdfs/google-cloud-security-and-compliance-whitepaper.pdf.
- Google's management performs periodic assessments of internal identity, authentication and source code management controls.

- Google has an established policy specifying that access to information resources, including data and the systems that store or process data, is authorized based on the principle of least privilege.
- Google maintains formal user registration and de-registration procedures for granting and revoking access.
- Google has established formal guidelines for passwords to govern the management and use of authentication mechanisms.
- Access to sensitive Google systems and applications requires two-factor authentication in the form of a user ID, password, security key and/or certificate.
- Google separates the duties of individuals by granting users access based on job responsibilities and least privilege and limiting access to only authorized users.
- Access to Google's production machines, support tools and network devices are managed via access control lists. Modifications of the access control lists are recorded and approved by administrators.
- Access to Google's corporate network, production machines, network devices and support tools requires a unique ID and verified credentials.
- Access to Google's network devices is authenticated via a user ID, password, security key and/or certificate.
- Only Google users with the authorized private key may gain SSH access to production machines.
- Access to Google's internal support tools is restricted to authorized personnel using approved credentials.
- External Google system users are identified and authenticated via the Google Accounts authentication system before access is granted.
- Remote access to corporate machines requires a Google-issued digital certificate installed on the connecting device and two-factor authentication in the form of a user ID, password, security key and/or certificate.
- Storage media used for offsite redundancy are protected and controlled during transport outside controlled areas using secure storage containers.

AWARENESS AND TRAINING

- Google has established a privacy and information security training programme and requires relevant personnel to complete this training annually.
- Google has a dedicated security team that is responsible for educating Google employees and contractors on security. Google has security policies that have been approved by management and published on the intranet, which are accessible to all employees and contractors.

- Privileged users understand their roles and responsibilities.
- Third-party stakeholders—that is, suppliers, customers and partners—understand their roles and responsibilities.
- Senior executives understand their roles and responsibilities.
- Physical and cybersecurity personnel understand their roles and responsibilities.

DATA SECURITY

- Multiple tenants are separated by individual databases and containers, such that there is no possibility for cross-contamination of data.
- Communications and data transfers to data stores are encrypted via TLS 1–1.2 protocols.
- Encryption is used for traffic traversing the fibre between Google production facilities.
- Google has an established key management process in place to support the organization's use of cryptographic techniques.
- Customer data that are uploaded or created are encrypted at rest.
- Passwords are stored in the Möbius database using a b-crypt encryption scheme.
- Databases are partially encrypted; that is, passwords are fully encrypted, but all table information is not fully encrypted.
- DigitalEd uses Google's Cloud Platform data centres as the hosts.
- There are three centres used, which are as follows:

  - North America data are hosted in Montreal, Canada.
  - European Union and UK data are hosted in Germany.
  - Australia and Japan data are hosted in Australia.

- Additionally, customers from China utilize Aliyun.

  - Chinese data are hosted in China.

- Anti-virus, phishing detection, secure coding and anti-malware/anti-spam tools are in place to protect Google's information assets. Tools are utilized to detect deviations from pre-defined OS configurations on production machines and correct them.
- PII on removable media leaving Google facilities is approved and encrypted.
- Google prohibits the use of removable media for the storage of PII and SPII unless the data have been encrypted.
- Google data centre server floors, network rooms and security systems are physically isolated from public spaces and/or delivery areas.

- Access to sensitive data centre zones requires approval from authorized personnel and is controlled via badge readers, biometric identification mechanisms and/or physical locks.
- Google data centres use redundant power systems and environmental controls for all systems to ensure reliability.

INFORMATION PROTECTION PROCESSES AND PROCEDURES

- Google has developed policies and procedures governing the secure development lifecycle.
- Google application and configuration changes are tested prior to implementation to production.
- Google system changes are reviewed and approved by a separate technical resource before moving into production.
- DigitalEd uses an application lifecycle management tool to manage all changes to the product and configuration changes. The process is reviewed every release and is followed by all engineering staff. The process has input from several stakeholders, as well as reviewers.
- Any changes to DigitalEd's policies or environment would be communicated directly to the appropriate contacts and via the following privacy policy page: www.digitaled.com/privacy.
- In the event of emergencies that may affect Möbius services, customer contact persons are notified immediately with any relevant information and resolution plans.
- DigitalEd can communicate by phone, e-mail and in application messaging via a banner.
- DigitalEd reviews and updates the BCP annually.
- In the event of emergencies that may affect Möbius services, backups (onsite and offsite) can be used to restore functionality in other locations with minimal loss of data.
- Each region listed below has three zones used to provide continuous service. However, data are maintained in the appropriate regions as follows:
  - North America data are hosted in Montreal, Canada.
  - European Union and UK data are hosted in Germany.
  - Australia and Japan data are hosted in Australia.
- DigitalEd is currently in the process of updating the Disaster Recovery Plan (DRP); once updated, it will be reviewed and tested.
- DigitalEd Engineering has a checklist of security-related questions and testing that is used to ensure that the product is securely developed and implemented.

- Google has security policies addressing confidentiality, integrity and availability that have been approved by management and published on the intranet, which is accessible to all employees.
- Google establishes security policies and procedures that clearly define the information security responsibilities of all employees. Within the information security policies and procedures, Google assigns responsibilities to the Google Information Security team.
- Google manages operational risk by delegating decisions regarding risk identification and resource prioritization to the various engineering groups that directly support the operation of Google products and services.
- Google has established policies and procedures that govern the use of cryptographic controls.

MAINTENANCE

- DigitalEd has a separate group known as the site reliability team that manages and maintains the systems that support Möbius.
- This team has several tools that are used to manage changes to the system and ensure that changes are reviewed and well understood.
- The maintenance and repair of assets are performed and logged with approved and controlled tools.
- Remote maintenance of assets is approved, logged and performed in a manner that prevents unauthorized access.

PROTECTIVE TECHNOLOGY

- Audit/log records are determined, documented, implemented and reviewed in accordance with policy.
- Removable media are protected, and their use is restricted according to policy.
- The principle of least functionality is incorporated by configuring systems to provide only essential capabilities.
- Communications and control networks are protected.
- Mechanisms—that is, failure safety, load balancing, and hot swaps—are implemented to achieve resilience requirements in normal and adverse situations.
- Mechanisms are in place to prevent and disconnect unauthorized access to the Google network from unauthorized devices.
- Google segregates networks based on the types of services, users and information systems.

- Google has an established key management process in place to support the organization's use of cryptographic techniques.
- Descriptions of Google's system and its boundaries are available to authorized external users by ongoing communications with customers or via Google's official blog postings.
- Google has dedicated teams who are responsible for monitoring, maintaining, managing and securing the networks. Access to network devices is restricted to authorized personnel and is periodically reviewed. Devices require a valid machine certificate to access the corporate network. Connections to the corporate wireless network are encrypted. There are mechanisms in place to protect the production environment against a variety of application-layer denial-of-service attacks.
- Google segregates networks based on the types of services, users and information systems.

ANOMALIES AND EVENTS

- A baseline of network operations and expected data flows for users and systems is established and managed.
- Detected events are analysed to understand attack targets and methods.
- Event data are collected and correlated from multiple sources and sensors.
- The impacts of events are determined.
- Incident alert thresholds are established.
- When Google determines that there has been a breach, policies and procedures exist to ensure that customers are notified in a timely manner in accordance with disclosure laws or contractual agreements.

SECURITY CONTINUOUS MONITORING

- DigitalEd has a policy of performing security and penetration testing annually, including incorporating the lessons learned into the software development life cycle.
- In November 2019, security penetration testing was performed by Info-Transec against the 2019.2 release.
- In situations when security/penetration testing vulnerabilities are identified, they are prioritized with the most critical problems addressed in the release.
- The network is monitored to detect potential cybersecurity events.
- The physical environment is monitored to detect potential cybersecurity events.
- Personnel activity is monitored to detect potential cybersecurity events.

- Malicious and unauthorized code detection is in place.
- External service provider activity is monitored to detect potential cybersecurity events.
- Monitoring for unauthorized personnel, connections, devices and software is performed.
- Cloud-based servers have numerous security teams and personnel onsite monitoring systems to provide 24 × 7 services.
- There are mechanisms in place to protect the Google production environment against a variety of application-layer denial-of-service attacks.
- Google has implemented a vulnerability management programme to detect and remediate system vulnerabilities.

DETECTION PROCESSES

- The roles and responsibilities for detection are well defined to ensure accountability.
- The detection activities comply with all applicable requirements.
- The detection processes are tested.
- Event detection information is communicated.
- The detection processes are continuously improved.
- Google has an established incident response policy that outlines the management responsibilities and procedures to ensure quick, effective and orderly responses to information security incidents.
- Monitoring tools send automated alerts to operational personnel based on predetermined criteria. Incidents are escalated per policy.

RESPONSE PLANNING

- The response plan is executed during or after an incident.
- Information security incidents are documented per Google's incident response policy. The information collected from these events is used to prevent future incidents and can be used as examples for information security training.

COMMUNICATIONS

- The personnel know their roles and order of operations when a response is needed.
- Incidents are reported consistent with established criteria.
- Information is shared consistent with the response plans.
- Coordination with stakeholders occurs consistent with the response plans.

- Voluntary information sharing occurs with external stakeholders to achieve broader cybersecurity situational awareness.

ANALYSIS

- Notifications from detection systems are investigated.
- The impact of the incident is understood.
- Forensics are performed.
- Incidents are categorized as consistent with the response plans.
- Processes are established to receive, analyse and respond to vulnerabilities disclosed to the organization from internal and external sources—that is, internal testing, security bulletins or security researchers.

MITIGATION

- Incidents are contained.
- Incidents are mitigated.
- Newly identified vulnerabilities are mitigated or documented as accepted risks.

RECOVERY PLANNING

- The recovery plan is executed during or after a cybersecurity incident.
- Google conducts DR testing on an annual basis to provide a coordinated venue for infrastructure and application teams to test communication plans, failover scenarios, operational transition and other emergency responses. All teams who participate in the DR exercise develop testing plans and post-mortems, which document the results and lessons learned from the tests.

IMPROVEMENTS

- The recovery plans incorporate the lessons learned.
- Recovery strategies are updated.

COMMUNICATIONS

- Public relations are managed.
- Reputation is repaired after an incident.
- Recovery activities are communicated to internal and external stakeholders, as well as executive and management teams.

Organization's risk appetite

The residual risk rating is MEDIUM LOW for the Möbius Platform.

Risk-mitigation strategy

Further risk-mitigation recommendations can be utilized to align with the business unit's risk profile and the NIST Cybersecurity Framework's core components.

Supplier chain risk management

- ABC University should ensure that Aliyun is routinely assessed using audits, test results or other forms of evaluations to confirm that they are meeting their contractual obligations.
- ABC University should ensure that response, recovery planning and testing are conducted with suppliers and third-party providers.

Identity management, authentication and access controls

- Existing technology and processes within ABC University should be reviewed, and appropriate security controls should be implemented to include integration with ABC University's LMS.
- The web-based interface should support authentication, including standard-based single sign-on (SSO), leveraging MFA and password/ passphrase ageing requirements.

Information protection processes and procedures

- DigitalEd should consider implementing an approved DR process documentation.
- All components of DigitalEd's DRP should be reviewed at least annually and updated as needed to reflect the change.
- PII-related information security controls:
    - Protect the transfer of data from ABC University to the cloud hosting environment—that is, Google, Alibaba.
    - Examples of secure application programmable interfaces (APIs), include the following:
        - Creation of accounts for client applications.
        - Account updates to use HTTP basic authentication.
        - Granularity of access control to ensure each client application has access to the functions it needs for the applicable operation.

- The database containing PII located within the cloud hosting environment should

  - protect PII elements—that is, encryption, masking and hashing;
  - provide reports for database logging of administrator/administrator-equivalent accounts for review by ABC University's management; and
  - implement integrity controls on database and system logs.

Awareness and training

- Implement ongoing training on and ensure that employees are aware of the appropriate handling and processing of PII and data privacy.

Security monitoring

- The ability to monitor for intrusions within the DigitalEd environment.
- Integration of security/data-related breach policies and procedures with ABC's incident management process.

Case study #2: Chime Live solution

As part of its 50th celebrations and in response to learner surveys, ABC University had two in-person convocation ceremonies planned for 2020: one at ABC on September 18 and another in Toronto on October 2. Due to the COVID-19 pandemic, ABC University made the difficult decision to cancel its in-person convocation ceremonies planned for 2020. Delivering an engaging and impactful convocation for ABC learners is an important foundational commitment to the university's learners and community. For this reason, the university selected Chime Live as a virtual event platform to host the 2020 convocation. ABC had an opportunity to reimagine the convocation in its 50th year in a way that would set it apart from other post-secondary institutions and truly highlight its "digital-first" mandate. The Chime Live platform would provide this opportunity, as it is a "virtual event" platform that enables live interactions among learners, guests and ABC team members.

In spring 2020, the world faced an unprecedented situation, with countries locked down, stay-at-home orders in place and, for the meetings and events industry, the inability to gather. Questions arose regarding the immediate need for virtual meetings. To help industry professionals bridge the gap, PSAV and its family of companies produced a global webcast on April 2, 2020, that featured a team of experts. The team described real-life applications and solutions for planning, producing and promoting a world-class virtual event from start to finish. The event included the following:

- Six hours of live broadcasting.
- Fifty-seven countries reached.
- Eight interactive sessions.
- Twenty remote presenters.
- Thirteen thousand people.

How it all came together: Traditional roles were transitioned to virtual roles with similar responsibilities. Multiple cross-functional teams came together from around the world to provide their specialized services, including production services, technical support, content development, creative design and speaker coaching.

Chime Live platform

ABC University selected Chime Live as a virtual event platform to host the 2020 convocation. The purpose of the Chime Live platform was to host and enhance the university's reimagined convocation in a way that would allow the university to celebrate with ABC learners and the ABC community. Chime Live is a stand-alone platform that will not be integrated with or connected to the ABC University-owned technology environment.

Chime Live connects remote presenters and participants with interactive features that assist in overcoming distractions and maintaining high engagement levels. At home, at work or at the venue, Chime Live simplifies the streaming process and easily broadcasts keynote presentations, topic streams and planned breakouts. The purpose of this solution is to enhance the learners' experience during the reimagined convocation ceremony by allowing some live interaction. This approach is consistent with learners' expectations for an in-person ceremony because it allows them to interact and connect with their fellow graduates.

The desired goals and supporting objectives for the convocation that would be realized as a result of utilizing Chime Live include the following:

1 Celebrate learners' accomplishments in a meaningful way in the 2020 ceremony:

   a Allow for graduate "real-time" networking by faculty or programme.
   b Include all undergraduate and graduate, as well as diploma and certificate programme, students.

Figure 8.2 Chime Live connects remote presenters and participants with interactive features.

2   Develop a virtual convocation experience that has impact and engagement and includes the following elements:

   a   Ceremony history and tradition.
   b   Focus on the attendee experience.
   c   Virtual reality tours of buildings and grounds.
   d   A congratulations video from the ABC team.

3   Include the following legacy items in celebration of ABC's 50th anniversary:

   a   Produce activations for a "festival"-type feel for the convocation, including a Beyond 50 installation (museum in a box), and feature virtual information booths for faculties, departments and centres.
   b   Create special graduation photo filters for graduate use.

c   Allow real-time congratulations on social walls, sharing of videos and pictures and the capturing of these pieces for historical purposes.

d   Include footage from the June 25, 2020, Light the Night event at ABC and the lighting of the High-level Bridge in Edmonton and the Calgary Tower in Calgary.

Access by PSAV employees to ABC data in the AWS infrastructure is granted as follows:

- Access to the AWS console is ACL restricted and requires MFA.
- Databases are encrypted at rest, and all database interactions are encrypted in transit.
- Database backups are stored encrypted.
- All encryption is accomplished using the AWS key management system.
- Access to encryption keys is restricted to authorized network administrators.
- Keys are rotated on an annual basis.
- Access to ABC data is restricted to authorized personnel using various access control systems.
- Access to systems is restricted to authorized personnel via encrypted virtual private network (VPN) access.

Questions

1   Determine the inherent risk.
2   Assess the internal control environment using the NIST Cybersecurity Framework: Core Components.
3   Determine the risk appetite, risk tolerance and risk profile.
4   Assess the residual risk and provide recommendations, if appropriate.
5   Develop the risk-mitigation strategy.

Case study #3: Marketing automation tool

Currently, ABC University's University Relation Department uses multiple tools, including but not limited to MailChimp, Unbounce and Sprout Social, to manage and track its marketing activities—that is, e-mail nurturing, landing pages and conversions, and social media posting to prospective students. It is difficult for recruitment, marketing and communication team members to coordinate their efforts due to the lack of an integrated view of this landscape. HubSpot Marketing Hub would solve this challenge by integrating marketing automation within a single-view experience. HubSpot Marketing Hub would be integrated with the Ellucian CRM Recruit product (ILE) to provide end-to-end management of prospective learners, including their behavioural interactions and experiences with ABC marketing and recruitment activities. HubSpot Marketing Hub would help meet campaign objectives, which include improving learner/stakeholder satisfaction, gaining a larger market share, and increasing operational efficiencies to drive learner applications and registrations.

The implementation of HubSpot Marketing Hub would allow ABC's marketing and recruitment efforts to scale efficiently as the University Relations Department continues to improve its ability to service faculties with programmatic and personalized marketing efforts. These strategies are currently under development and are aligned with ABC's imagine strategy, the University Relations Department's goals and the enrolment/growth targets outlined in ABC's strategic enrolment management (SEM) plan.

HubSpot is the world's leading inbound marketing, sales and services platform. Since 2006, it has progressively moved towards the globalization of its solution. Today, tens of thousands of customers in more than 90 countries use HubSpot software, services and support to transform the way they attract, engage and serve customers. HubSpot's inbound marketing software is ranked #1 by VentureBeat, GetApp, Capterra and G2Crowd and includes social media publishing and monitoring, blogging, search engine optimization (SEO), website content management, e-mail marketing and reporting and analytics in one integrated platform.

HubSpot Sales Hub and CRM, HubSpot's award-winning sales applications, enable sales and service teams to have more effective conversations with leads, prospects and customers. HubSpot Service Hub is the best solution for creating a frictionless environment and satisfying customer experiences.

HubSpot products are offered as SAS solutions. These solutions are available to the university through purpose-built web applications, APIs and e-mail plug-ins.

The primary benefactor of the HubSpot investment would be ABC's marketing and student recruitment teams, as this would help them improve their ability to strategically serve prospective learners.

Business functionality

The HubSpot Marketing Hub provided ABC with inclusive inbound marketing software that facilitates the following activities:

1 Development of content.
2 Targeted online traffic.
3 The ability to identify potential customers.
4 Tracking and reporting of consumer behaviour.
5 Provision of a software-based tool to organize and manage information internally.

Table 8.3 The Marketing Hub features

Marketing Hub (built on HubSpot CRM) Features

Forms	Mobile Optimization	Phone Support	Sub-domain Availability	Custom Reporting
Ad Management	User Roles	Blog & Content Creation Tools	Marketing Automation	Campaign Reporting
Conversations Inbox	Messenger Integration	SEO & Content Strategy	Salesforce Integration	Website Traffic Analytics
Team E-mail	Landing Pages	Google Search Console Integration	Smart Content	Calculated Properties
Live Chat	Ad Retargeting	Social Media	Attribution Reporting	Hierarchical Teams
Conversational Bot	Custom Properties	Calls to Action	A/B Testing	Custom Event Triggers and Reporting
E-mail Marketing	Multiple Currencies	Standard SSL Certificate	Video Hosting & Management	Event-Based Segmentation
List Segmentation	Record Customization	Competitor	Team	Predictive Lead Scoring
SSO	Partitioning	CMS Membership	E-mail Send Frequency Cap	YouTube integration
Social Permissions	Filtered Analytics View	Events API	Multi-touch Revenue Attribution	Adaptive Testing

Questions

1   Determine the inherent risk.
2   Assess the internal control environment using the NIST Cybersecurity Framework: Core Components.
3   Determine the risk appetite, risk tolerance and risk profile.
4   Assess the residual risk and provide recommendations, if appropriate.
5   Develop the risk-mitigation strategy.

Case study #4: CatchMyData

Current state

CatchMyData is a third-party organization that is contracted by ABC University IT Services (ITS) to collect data from ABC's student financial aid course registration plan form. The long-term relationship with CatchMyData extends over 10 years and is managed through the Office of the Registrar for the loan study plan application. A privacy impact assessment (PIA) was completed by the ABC Privacy Office and indicated that PII is captured and stored through this web application. The data collected through this form are sent to CatchMyData for management within one backend database. The database is located within a secure data centre managed by Alentus and located in the Edmonton Rogers Data Centre. Initially, the loan study plan front-end web application was developed and managed by the university approximately 10 years earlier.

The data captured by CatchMyData are collected from a historical university-created and -managed web page, the course registration plan (a.k.a. loan study plan). PII-relevant items collected from the applicant are defined by the university for its own use. The user-identifiable items are the name, address, phone number, e-mail, SIN, ABC ID and provincial ID as submitted by the applicant.

CatchMyData does not share or distribute these data. All changes to the data captured are at the discretion and direction of the ABC Student Loan Office. The captured data are stored in a distinct and separate database and are not commingled with any other CatchMyData client data. The ABC client application provided by CatchMyData is accessed through a TLS v.1.2 encrypted session, where the login name and password are transmitted for ABC Student Loan Office users.

PII data are stored in a third-party secure cloud service in Canada, and access to the server is restricted to two distinct IP addresses, with no access by third-party organizations. ABC users are provided access by the administrator, Barrie Jackson, or the manager, Valmir Oppenager. The student financial aid advisor logins in CatchMyData are created and administered by Barrie Jackson, who is the sole individual from ABC University with administrative privileges to this database.

User access is granted through the ABC University IT access policy, and access is granted based on a user's job function within the university. Therefore, any changes to either the administrator or manager role would be authorized directly by ABC University's management.

Future state

The change proposed by the university was to renovate the course registration plan page to facilitate adaption to course changes and session timing more rapidly. Structural changes to the course registration plan were proposed using CatchMyData's smart form. The application code used to capture the data would remain largely intact, as originally created by ABC, and would be maintained within the CatchMyData environment. CatchMyData as a company would continue to abide by the original ABC contract in terms of security, application maintenance and backup.

Questions

1 Determine the inherent risk.
2 Assess the internal control environment using the NIST Cybersecurity Framework: Core Components.
3 Determine the risk appetite, risk tolerance and risk profile.
4 Assess the residual risk and provide recommendations, if appropriate.
5 Develop the risk-mitigation strategy.

Case study #5: Moneris Solutions

SAD refers to the information on a payment card used for authentication at the time of a purchase, including data from the full magnetic strip, card security code (CSC, CVV2, CID, CAV2) and PIN. Within the payment card processing model, ABC University has a merchant relationship with its acquiring bank for accepting payment card transactions. ABC University has outsourced the transaction processing of payment card data to a third-party service provider, Moneris Solutions. The university's vendor is responsible for compliance with regulatory and legal statutes, as well as protecting such information from dissemination to unauthorized parties. This risk-assessment report provides the residual risk profile for the credit card service fee model project.

The university has an existing relationship with Moneris Solutions to provide transaction processing for ABC customers. The current relationship is detailed here.

Figure 8.3 The Moneris Solution transaction processing process for customers.

The hosted pay page (HPP) process flow is as follows:

1   The customer arrives on the ABC University website (application). At this point, the university must determine the amount of the transaction and collect any additional data.
2   Once the cardholder is ready to pay, the university checkout page will submit an HTTP form POST to the Moneris HPP. At this time, the customer will be redirected from the university website to the Moneris HPP URL.
3   On the HPP, the cardholder will provide secure payment details, such as the card number, and submit the transaction. At this time, Moneris will process the transaction and then provide a receipt to the customer.
4   Once the customer is ready to continue, he or she will be redirected back to the university website to the response URL provided in the HPP configuration.

The change that is being proposed by the university is to add service fees—specifically, convenience fees—to the university receipt. The convenience fee programme was designed to allow merchants to offer the convenience of an alternative payment channel to the cardholder at a charge. This applies only when providing a true "convenience" in the form of an alternative payment channel. The convenience fee is a separate charge on top of what the consumer is paying for the goods and/or services being purchased, and this charge will appear as a separate line item on the consumer's statement. From an information security viewpoint, the impact of this change is minimal. It was confirmed that a PIA was not required, as PII was not within the scope of this project enhancement. In addition, the new receipt would not contain any sensitive data that would require additional security controls within the university. The university maintained its current transaction processing relationship through the service provider Moneris Solutions.

Questions

1   Determine the inherent risk.
2   Assess the internal control environment using the NIST Cybersecurity Framework: Core Components.
3   Determine the risk appetite, risk tolerance and risk profile.
4   Assess the residual risk and provide recommendations, if appropriate.
5   Develop the risk-mitigation strategy.

Case study #6: Alumni Learning Consortium

The Alumni Learning Consortium (ALC) is a new webinar platform designed to meet the specific needs of alumni associations. The University of Maryland and 11 other colleges and universities formed the ALC, which is managed by Professional Book Club Guru (PBC Guru).

Current initiative

The ALC is an organization that can assist ABC University with creating online programmes to drive alumni engagement. ABC University partnered with PBC Guru to utilize the CloudWays web hosting platform. This solution provides the university with an ABC-branded website that facilitates content management and delivery to ABC alumni for the following services:

1   *Livestream platforms* – hosted webinars and live-stream events to international participants, with a limitless number of events or participants, including the following:

- Unlimited events, registrations and viewers.
- A school-branded microsite that allows alumni to register for upcoming live streams, view live streams and watch past events.
- Analytics of the individuals who register and attend each programme.
- Personalized screen views that allow on-screen branding with support for webinars, panel discussions and streaming in-person events.
- Seamless integration with white-label live streams created by the ALC.
- An annual fund donation request on the registration page of each online event.
- Technical support and platform training.

2   *White-label webinars*—programming from best-selling authors and career experts for alumni at all life stages. The ALC produces two to four webinars per month that are open to the alumni of all member schools. These webinars cover a range of career, life-stage and life-long learning topics to engage different segments of ABC alumni. Each webinar is "white labelled", meaning that it is branded for ABC on the alumni webinar page, creating a seamless watch experience for ABC alumni. The consortium can bring top presenters to the ABC alumni due to the size of the ALC network.

3 *Professional society*—connect with other consortium members to learn best practices to develop professionally.
4 *Expert support*—specifically designed for alumni associations to succeed.

Managed service provider (MSP) model

PBC Guru utilizes the cloud hosting platform offered through CloudWays to provide development, content delivery and operations of the ABC-branded website. CloudWays utilizes secure data centres managed by Digital Realty Data Centre Services, and Data Centre NYC3 houses the technology to support this solution. ABC University is responsible for managing, updating and maintaining the ABC ALC website. Therefore, ABC has dedicated site administrators to providing overall management for the ABC ALC website.

Questions

1 Determine the inherent risk.
2 Assess the internal control environment using the NIST Cybersecurity Framework: Core Components.
3 Determine the risk appetite, risk tolerance and risk profile.
4 Assess the residual risk and provide recommendations, if appropriate.
5 Develop the risk-mitigation strategy.

Case study #7: Cascade software

ABC University is a semi-virtual organization, and learners, staff and other stakeholder groups are reliant upon user interfaces (websites) to access online information and resources—that is, courses, programmes and services. The usability and effectiveness of these interfaces, including the quality of their digital content, are paramount in establishing an effective digital experience. However, the university's current digital experience has become increasingly fragmented. In addition, the web publishing functionality in its existing solution (Alfresco Web Content Management) is no longer offered or supported by the vendor, and a scalable cloud-based solution is required to support the achievement of the university's strategic goals. This risk assessment was intended to review the changes to content management and content delivery functions associated with the Cascade initiative. Any existing processes would be out of scope for this assessment, which included but was not limited to the identity and access management process that utilized the university's

SSO authentication mechanism. It is important to note that sensitive data are not intentionally stored within the CMS hosting architecture.

The Cascade initiative would perform the following:

- Implement a new DX platform and DNS server in ABC's cloud for Internet and intranet publishing requirements.
- Develop a new scalable and high-availability architecture for ABC's Internet and intranet, including a monitoring mechanism to gauge performance.
- Develop an Internet and intranet site redesign and implementation plan that includes approaches to audit existing sites, develop criteria to identify "high-value sites", develop and implement SEO tactics and work with stakeholders to redesign and deploy (or decommission and archive) primary sites based on the new web design and publishing standards and workflows.
- Integrate website improvement and digital asset management (DAM) tools with the DX platform via APIs and configuration.
- Rationalize and classify all identified sites.
- Redesign and deploy new sites deemed "high-value" primary sites and decommission and/or archive the old sites.
- Develop a list of secondary and tertiary sites for future redesign and deployment with the redesign of secondary and tertiary sites being out of scope.
- Establish analytics—that is, Google Analytics—for all primary websites deployed.

The application has two components: content management and content delivery. The former is a publishing engine that distributes content to a user-defined target. The latter is an arbitrary solution that is utilized by the Cascade software product to provide web content to an audience that is most appropriate to the business.

The websites are categorized based on a criticality rating:

- Critical—medium volume (10,000+), tied to event or business process or important communications asset.
- Important—low-volume (<10,000) occasional use, not critical to move and can wait.
- Non-critical—faculty web content for current students and staff.
- LSS—low volume does not support a business process; however, it may contain historical information.
- Out of scope—high volume (50,000+) used daily—students and staff.

The Cascade web content management system provides a means to publish information about ABC University's academic resources for students and faculty and employment resources for staff. University websites are the primary means for communication with the audience; therefore, this is a business-critical application. The following services for website indexing, site search capabilities and DAM were included within this project:

1   SiteSearch360—Batman Option as an alternative to the Google Mini Search Appliance. The owner of this service is SEMKNOX GmbH, and it involves the insertion of simple JavaScript into the Cascade website to facilitate search capabilities—specifically, four lines of code. Therefore, hosting or vendor involvement is out of scope. Site Search 360 has attained various industry requirements, as follows:

   - PCI DSS compliance.
   - ISO/IEC 27001:2013 for data centre certification.
   - The data processing agreement (DPA) required by general data protection regulations (GDPR).
   - Technical and organizational measures from SEMKNOX GmbH, the legal entity behind Site Search 360, and Hoster.

2   The Enterprise DAM solution utilizes an outsourced data centre managed by Brandfolder, and its features include the ability to perform the following:

   - Tag and categorize assets.
   - Manage asset metadata—that is, name, date and description.
   - Create a workflow—that is, permissions for internal and external audiences, reviews and approvals, and notification.
   - Implement version control and rights management—that is, user restrictions.
   - Implement asset sharing across various teams—that is, lightboxes and asset tracking.
   - Perform searches—that is, simple and advanced searches in the DAM.
   - Edit assets—that is, images within the DAM—and convert to different formats.
   - Replace an asset in the DAM and have the replacement changed on the website.
   - Create a gallery within the DAM.
   - Implement reporting.

The university does not intentionally store sensitive or classified information on the web content management system. However, the possibility of accidental storage and distribution of this type of information exists.

Questions

1 Determine the inherent risk.
2 Assess the internal control environment using the NIST Cybersecurity Framework: Core Components.
3 Determine the risk appetite, risk tolerance and risk profile.
4 Assess the residual risk and provide recommendations, if appropriate.
5 Develop the risk-mitigation strategy.

Case study #8: Chrome River travel and expense

The purpose of this risk assessment was to assess the risk associated with implementing Module Finance Upgrade Phase 2: Travel and Expense Claim Module. Sensitive ABC data are collected, transmitted and stored in this system, and the risk assessment reviews the controls in place to adequately protect ABC data as required by the university's data classification standard operating procedure.

Chrome River applications leverage years of security leadership to utilize (1) security by design, achieved through multilayer encryption capabilities, secure systems framework and annual risk analysis; (2) enforced standards, tested processes and dedicated tools to protect customer data; and (3) annual security education and certification for employees to comply with established business conduct guidelines. Operational security is enforced by state-of-the-art scanning and intrusion detection, continuously updated to stay ahead of new attack vectors. Chrome River conducts regular audits to verify that operational security meets control requirements and that a global security incident process is in place that is monitored 24 hours per day, 7 days a week and 365 days per year ($24{\times}7{\times}365$). Chrome River services are designed to protect proprietary ABC content and data.

In April 2018, ABC began the Module Finance & HR Upgrade Project to upgrade the finance, payroll and position control modules from Module version 8 to Module version 9, as Ellucian was removing support for Module version 8 at the end of 2018. This phase of the project specifically included only the core modules, and items such as the Travel and Expense Management System (Module TEM) were listed as out of scope. The project team successfully implemented this upgrade in November 2018.

With the core finance and HR modules upgraded to supported versions, the finance and administration departments examined the support status of the out-of-scope modules in the project. Module TEM entered sustaining support status on January 1, 2019. Ellucian's supported expense management solution became Chrome River expense management, and the project sponsor requested that an upgrade to this module be included as a second phase of the Module Finance & HR Upgrade project. Digital governance approved a project change request in February 2019 to implement the Chrome River expense management and invoice management modules. The legacy module TEM and associated module workflow products were be decommissioned.

The purpose of this project was to implement the Module Finance Upgrade Phase 2: Travel and Expense Claim Module.

Questions

1   Determine the inherent risk.
2   Assess the internal control environment using the NIST Cybersecurity Framework: Core Components.
3   Determine the risk appetite, risk tolerance and risk profile.
4   Assess the residual risk and provide recommendations, if appropriate.
5   Develop the risk-mitigation strategy.

Bibliography

Alali, M., Almogren, A., Hassan, M. M., Rassan, I. A. L. & Bhuiyan, M. Z. A. 2018. Improving risk assessment model of cyber security using fuzzy logic inference system. *Computer & Security*, 74, 323–339.

Albrechtsen, E. & Howden, J. 2009. The information security digital divide between information security managers and users. *Computer & Security*, 28, 476–490.

Alexiou, S. 2019. Practical patch management and mitigation. *ISACA Journal*, 3.

Alkaabi, A. 2014. *Strategic Framework to Minimize Information Security Risks in the UAE*. PhD, University of Bedfordshire.

Avgerou, C. 2000. Information systems: What sort of science is it? *Omega* (West-Port), 28, 567–579.

AWS. 2019. Native container image scanning in Amazon ECR (AWS, 2019), viewed March 2020, aws.amazon.com/blogs/containers/amazon-ecr-native-container-image-scanning.

Bang, S. K., Chung, S., Choh, Y. & Dupuis, M. 2013. *A Grounded Theory Analysis of Modern Web Applications: Knowledge, Skills, and Abilities for DevOps*. Information Technology & Systems, Institute of Technology, University of Washington, Tacoma.

Baranyi, J. & Buss da Silva, N. 2017. The use of predictive models to optimize risk of decisions. *International Journal of Food Microbiology*, 240, 19–23.

Basel Committee on Banking Supervision. 2001. *Operational Risk, Banking for International Settlement*.

Bin Ishaq Alseiari, K. 2015. *The Management of Risk Awareness in Relation to Information Technology (MERIT)*. PhD, University of Gloucestershire.

Birks, M. & Mills, J. 2015. *Grounded Theory: A Practical Guide*. London, UK: SAGE Publication.

Bojanc, R. & Jerman-Blazic, B. 2008. An economic modelling approach to information security risk management. *International Journal of Information Management*, 28, 413–22.

Bojanc, R., Jerman-Blažič, B. & Tekavčič, M. 2012. Managing the investment in information security technology by use of a quantitative modelling. *Information Processing & Management*, 48, 1031–1052.

Borgonovo, E., Cappelli, V., Maccheroni, F. & Marinacci, M. 2018. Risk analysis and decision theory: A bridge. *European Journal of Operational Research*, 264, 280–293.

Caldas, A. 2006. The Sergio Galanti Operational Risk Puzzle, viewed March 2020, www.riskmanagementguru.com/operational-risk/risk-puzzle

Campos, J., Sharma, P., Jantunen, E., Baglee, D., Fumagalli, L. & Slotwiner, D. J. 2016. The challenges of cybersecurity frameworks to protect data required for the development of advanced maintenance. *Procedia CIRP*, 47, 222–227.

Caralli, R., Stevens, J., Young, L. & Wilson, W. 2007. *Introducing OCTAVE Allegro: Improving the Information Security Risk Assessment Process*. Carnegie Mellon, USA.

Carty, M., Pimont, V. & Schmid, D. 2012. *Measuring the Value of Information Security Investments*. IT@Intel White Paper.

Cavusoglu, H., Mishra, B. & Ragunathan, S. 2004. A model for evaluating IT security investments. *ACM*, 47, 87–92.

Cavusoglu, H., Raghunathan, S. & Raghunathan, W. 2008. Decision-theoretic and game-theoretic approaches to IT security investment. *Management Information System*, 25, 281–304.

Cherdantseva, Y., Hilton, J., Rana, O. & Ivins, W. 2016. A multifaceted evaluation of the reference model of information assurance & security. *Computer & Security*, 63, 45–66.

Cho, S. 2003. *Risk Analysis and Management for Information Security*. PhD, Royal Holloway, University of London.

Comes, T., Hiete, M., Wijngaards, N. & Schultmann, F. 2011. Decision maps: A framework for multi criteria decision support under severe uncertainty. *Decision Support System*, 52, 108–118.

Committee of Sponsoring Organizations of the Treadway Commission. Viewed March 2020, www.coso.org.

Cremonini, M. & Nizovtsev, D. 2006. *Understanding and Influencing Attackers' Decisions: Implications for Security Investment Strategies*. Presented at the Workshop on the Economics of Information Security, June 26–28, 2006, Cambridge, England.

de Bruijn, H. & Janssen, M. 2017. Building cybersecurity awareness: The need for evidence-based framing strategies. *Government Information Quarterly*, 34, 1–7.

Digital Maelstrom. 2020. The elements within the secure software development lifecycle, viewed March 2020, www.digitalmaelstrom.net/it-security-services/secure-software-development-lifecycle-ssdlc.

Dildy, T. 2017. Enterprise vulnerability management. *ISACA Journal*, 2.

Dor, D. & Elovici, Y. 2016. A model of the information security investment decision-making process. *Computer & Security*, 63, 1–13.

Dresner, D. G. 2011. *A Study of Standards and the Mitigation of Risk in Information Systems*. PhD, University of Manchester.

Dutta, A. & Mccrohan, K. 2002. Management's role in information security in a cyber economy. *California Management*, 45, 67–87.

Easterby-Smith, M., Thorpe, R. & Jackson, P. R. 2015. *Management & Business Research*. London, UK: Sage.

Ericson, C. A. I. 2005. *Hazard Analysis Techniques for System Safety*. John Wiley & Sons.

European Union Agency for Networks and Information Security, Octave v2.0. Viewed May 2020, www.enisa.europa.eu.

Farroha, B. S. & Farroha, D. L. 2014. *A Framework for Managing Mission Needs, Compliance and Trust in the DevOps Environment.* 2014 IEEE Military Communications Conference.

Fazlida, M. R. & Said, J. 2015. Information security: Risk, governance and implementation setback. *Procedia Economics and Finance,* 28, 243–248.

Feng, N., Wang, H. J. & Li, M. 2014. A security risk analysis model for information systems causal relationships of risk factors and vulnerability propagation analysis. *Information Science,* 256, 57–73.

Fiegenbaum, A. & Thomas, H. 1988. Attitudes toward risk and the risk-return paradox: Prospect theory explanations. *Academy of Management Journal,* 32, 85–106.

Fielder, A., Panaousis, E., Malacaria, P., Hankin, C. & Smeraldi, F. 2013. Decision support approaches for cyber security investment. *Decision Support Systems,* 86, 13–23.

Finne, T. 1998. A conceptual framework for information security management. *Computer & Security,* 17, 303–307.

Garvey, P. R. 2008. *Analytical Methods for Risk Management: A Systems Engineering Perspective.* Boca Raton, London and New York: Chapman-Hall/CRC-Press, Taylor & Francis Group.

Ge, X.-Y., Yuan, Y.-Q. & Lu, L.-L. 2011. An information security maturity evaluation mode. *Procedia Engineering,* 24, 335–339.

Gordon, L. A. & Loeb, M. P. 2002. The economics of information security investment. *ACM Transactions on Information and System Security,* 5, 438–457.

Gordon, L. A. & Loeb, M. P. 2006. *Managing Cyber-Security Resources: A Cost-Benefit Analysis.* McGraw-Hill.

Gordon, L. A., Loeb, M. P. & Lucyshyn, W. 2003. Sharing information on computer systems security: An economic analysis. *Journal of Accounting and Public Policy,* 2, 461–485.

Gordon, L. A., Loeb, M. P., Lucyshyn, W. & Zhou, L. 2015. The impact of information sharing on cybersecurity underinvestment: A real options perspective. *Journal of Accounting and Public Policy,* 34, 509–519.

Gordon, L. A., Loeb, M. P. & Zhou, L. 2016. Investing in cybersecurity: Insights from the Gordon-Loeb model. *Journal of Information Security,* 7, 49–59.

Greene, F. 2015. Cybersecurity detective controls: Monitoring to identify and respond to threats. *ISACA Journal,* 5.

Grunske, L. & Joyce, D. 2008. Quantitative risk-based security prediction for component-based systems with explicitly modeled attack profiles. *The Journal of Systems and Software,* 81, 1327–1345.

Hausenblas, M. & Nguyen, R. 2019. *Native Container Image Scanning in Amazon ECR.* Amazon Web Services (AWS).

Henriques de Gusmão, A. P., Camara e Silva, L., Silva, M. M., Poleto, T. & Costa, A. P. C. S. 2016. Information security risk analysis model using fuzzy decision theory. *International Journal of Information Management,* 26, 25–34.

Huang, C. D. & Behara, R. S. 2013. Economics of information security investment in the case of concurrent heterogeneous attacks with budget constraints. *International Journal of Production Economics*, 141, 255–268.

Huang, C. D., Hu, Q. & Behara, R. S. 2008. An economic analysis of the optimal information security investment in the case of a risk-averse firm. *International Journal of Production Economics*, 114, 793–704.

Humble, J. & Molesky, J. 2011. Why DevOps must adopt continuous delivery to enable continuous delivery? *The Journal of Information Technology Management*, 24(8), 6–12.

Huntsman. 2017. *ASD Essential Eight: Patching and Vulnerability Management – How to Get it Right*. Viewed March–May 2020, www.huntsmansecurity.com.

Information Systems Audit and Control Association (ISACA). 2009. *The Risk IT Framework*. Viewed April 2020, www.isaca.org.

Information Systems Audit and Control Association (ISACA). 2017. *Vulnerability Assessment*. Viewed April 2020, www.isaca.org.

International Standards Organization (ISO). Viewed March–May 2020, www.iso.org.

Jegers, M. 1991. Prospect theory and the risk-return relation: Some Belgian evidence. *Academy of Management Journal*, 34, 215–225.

Johnson, A. 2009. Business and security executives' view of information security investment drivers: Results from a dephi study. *Information Privacy Security*, 5, 3–27.

Joshi, C. & Singh, U. K. 2017. Information security risks management framework: A step towards mitigating security risks in university network. *Journal of Information Security and Applications*, 35, 128–137.

Jouini, M., Rabai, L. B. A. & Khedri, R. 2015. A multidimensional approach towards a quantitative assessment of security threats. *Procedia Computer Science*, 52, 507–514.

Kemkhadze, N. 2004. *Information and Optimisation in Investment and Risk Measurement*. PhD, University of Warwick, Warwick Business School.

Kissoon, T. 2020. Optimum spending on cybersecurity measures. Emerald Publishing Ltd.: *Transforming Government: People, Process and Policy*, 14, 417–431.

Kissoon, T. 2021. Optimum spending on cybersecurity measures: Part II. *Journal of Information Security*, (Vol.12 No.1, Jan 2021).

Kolkowska, E., Karlsson, F. & Hedström, K. 2017. Towards analysing the rationale of information security non-compliance: Devising a value-based compliance analysis method. *The Journal of Strategic Information Systems*, 26, 39–57.

Kossiakoff, A. & Sweet, W. N. 2003. *Systems Engineering Principles and Practice*. John Wiley and Sons, Inc., pp. 98–106.

Lavine, M. K. 2007. *Cyber Security Information Sharing in the United States: An Empirical Study Including Risk Management and Control Implications, 2000–2003*. PhD, City University London.

Lee, S., Kim, S., Choi, K. & Shon, T. 2017. Game theory-based security vulnerability quantification for social internet of things. *Future Generation Computer Systems*, 1–9.

Lee, Y. J., Kauffman, R. J. & Sougstad, R. 2011. Profit maximizing firm investments in customer information security. *Decision Support Systems*, 51, 904–920.

Leuprecht, C., Skillicorn, D. B. & Tait, V. E. 2016. Beyond the Castle model of cyber-risk and cyber-security. *Government Information Quarterly*, 33, 250–257.

Lundberg, K. & Warvsten, A. 2020. *Automated Fuzzy Logic Risk Assessment and Its Role in a DevOps Workflow*. Master's Thesis, Lund University, Department of Computer Science.

ManageEngine. 2020. The patch management lifecycle, viewed March 2020, www.manageengine.ca.

Mayadunne, S. & Park, S. 2016. An economic model to evaluate information security investment of risk-taking small and medium enterprises. *International Journal of Production Economics*, 182, 519–530.

The MITRE Institute. 2007. *MITRE Systems Engineering (SE) Competency Model, Version 1*, pp. 10, 40–41.

Mortazavi-Alavi, R. 2016. *A Risk-driven Investment Model for Analysing Human Factors in Information Security*. PhD, University of East London.

Mukhopadhyay, A., Chatterjee, S., Saha, D., Mahanti, A. & Sadhukhan, S. K. 2013. Cyber-risk decision models: To insure IT or not? *Decision Support Systems*, 56, 1–26.

National Cyber Security Centre. 2016. *Summary of Risk Metods and Frameworks*. United Kingdom.

National Institute of Standards and Technology (NIST). Viewed March–May 2020, www.nist.gov.

Nazareth, D. & Choi, J. 2015. A system dynamics model for information security management. *Information Management*, 52, 123–34.

Ochoa, D. C. R., Correia, R., Peña, J. I. & Población, J. 2015. Expropriation risk, investment decisions and economic sectors. *Economic Modelling*, 48, 326–342.

Optiv. 2011. Residual risk rating scale, viewed March 2020, www.optiv.com.

Orojloo, H. & Azgomi, M. A. 2017. A game-theoretic approach to model and quantify the security of cyber-physical systems. *Computers in Industry*, 88, 44–57.

Palmaers, T. 2013. *Implementing a Vulnerability Management Process*. SANS Institute.

Pettigrew, A. 2009. *The Politics of Organizational Decision-Making*. Routledge.

Posey, C., Roberts, T. L., Lowry, P. B. & Hightower, R. T. 2014. Bridging the divide: A qualitative comparison of information security thought patterns between information security professionals and ordinary organizational insiders. *Information & Management*, 51, 551–567.

Purser, S. A. 2004. Improving the ROI of the security management process. *Computer Security*, 23, 542–546.

Rahimian, F., Bajaj, A. & Bradley, W. 2016. Estimation of deficiency risk and prioritization of information security controls: A data-centric approach. *International Journal of Accounting Information Systems*, 20, 38–64.

Rhee, H. S., Ryu, Y. U. & Kim, C.-T. 2012. Unrealistic optimism on information security management. *Computer & Security*, 31, 221–232.

Ringland, G. 2002. *Scenarios in Business*. John Wiley & Sons.

Rodriguez, E. 2010. *Knowledge Management Applied to Enterprise Risk Management*. PhD, Aston University.

Roldán-Molina, G., Almache-Cueva, M., Silva-Rabadão, C., Yevseyeva, I., & Basto-Fernandes, V. 2017. A comparison of cybersecurity risk analysis tools. Centeris – International Conferences on Enterprise Information Systems, 2017 Barcelona, Spain. *Procedia Computer Science*, 121, 568–575.

Rose, S., Spinks, N. & Canhoto, A. I. 205. *Management Research: Applying the Principles*. Abingdon, Oxon: Routledge.

Rue, R., Pfleeger, S. & Ortiz, D. 2007. *A Framework for Classifying and Comparing Models of Cyber Security Investment to Support Policy and Decision-making*. The Sixth Workshop on the Economics of Information Security (WEIS07).

Ryan, J. J. C. H., Mazzuchi, T. A., Ryan, D. J., Lopez de la Cruz, J. & Cooke, R. 2012. Quantifying information security risks using expert judgment elicitation. *Computers & Operations Research*, 39, 774–784.

Saleh, M. S. & Alfantookh, A. 2015. A new comprehensive framework for enterprise information security risk management. *Procedia Economics and Finance*, 28, 243–248.

Shameli-Sendi, A., Aghababaei-Barzegar, R. & Cheriet, M. 2016. Taxonomy of information security risk assessment (ISRA). *Computer & Security*, 57, 14–30.

Sharkasi, O. 2015. Addressing cybersecurity vulnerabilities. *ISACA Journal*, 5.

SmartSheet. 2020. Elements of the system development life-cycle, viewed March 2020, www.smartsheet.com/system-development-life-cycle.

Standards Australia. 2006. HB 167:2006 Security risk management. Sydney: Standards Australia International Ltd.

Tsiakis, T. & Stephanides, G. 2005. The economic approach of information security. *Computer & Security*, 24, 105–108.

van Schaik, P., Jeske, D., Onibokun, J., Coventry, L., Jansen, J. & Kusev, P. 2017. Risk perceptions of cyber-security and precautionary behaviour. *Computers in Human Behaviour*, 75.

van Staalduinen, M. A., Khan, F., Gadag, V. & Reniers, G. 2017. Functional quantitative security risk analysis (QSRA) to assist in protecting critical process infrastructure. *Reliability Engineering & System Safety*, 157, 23–24.

von Neuman, J. & Morgenster, O. 2007. *Theory of Games and Economic Behaviour*. Princeton, NJ: Princeton University Press.

von Solms, R. & van Niekerk, J. 2008. From information security to cyber security. *Computer & Security*, 38, 97–102.

WEBB, J., Ahmad, A., Maynard, S. B. & Shanks, G. 2014. A situation awareness model for information security risk management. *Computer & Security*, 57, 14–30.

Wiseman, R. M. & Gormez-Mejia, L. R. 1998. A behavioural agency model of managerial risk taking. *Academy of Management Review*, 23, 133–153.

Wu, Y., Feng, G., Wang, N. & Liang, H. 2015. Game of information security investment: Impact of attack types and network vulnerability. *Expert Systems with Applications*, 42, 6132–6146.

Wynn, J. 2014. *Threat Assessment and Remediation Analysis (TARA)*. Mitre Corporation.

Yevseyeva, I., Morisset, C. & van Moorsel, A. 2016. Modeling and analysis of influence power for information security decisions. *Performance Evaluation*, 98, 36–51.

Zavgorodniy, V., Lukyanov, P. & Nazarov, S. 2014. The selection algorithm of mechanisms for management of information risks. *Procedia Computer Science*, 31.

Index

Note: Page numbers in *italics* indicate a figure and page numbers in **bold** indicate a table on the corresponding page.